IMAGES
of America

FREDERICK
& NELSON

Clark Pounds, Frederick & Nelson's original doorman, was the friendly face of the store for more than four decades. In this *c.* 1940 photograph, he greets a customer at the main entrance to the store. Dressed to the nines in her stylish hat and white gloves, she might very well be on her way to a fashion show in the Tea Room. (Courtesy Wendell family.)

ON THE COVER: This iconic image of Frederick & Nelson shows the store at the close of its 75th anniversary year in 1965. That year the store received more fan mail than it had any previous Christmas. One customer wrote, "Every year Frederick's is lovely to behold, and all Seattleites look forward eagerly wondering what spectacular decorations will greet . . . shoppers . . . Fredericks's is my favorite store all year long every year, but even more so when it is decorated for Christmas." (Courtesy Frederick & Nelson Records, Museum of History and Industry, Seattle.)

IMAGES
of America

FREDERICK
& NELSON

Ann Wendell

ARCADIA
PUBLISHING

Published by Arcadia Publishing
Charleston SC, Chicago IL, Portsmouth NH, San Francisco CA

Printed in the United States of America

Library of Congress Catalog Card Number: 2008934523

For all general information contact Arcadia Publishing at:
Telephone 843-853-2070
Fax 843-853-0044
E-mail sales@arcadiapublishing.com
For customer service and orders:
Toll-Free 1-888-313-2665

Visit us on the Internet at www.arcadiapublishing.com

*To Abiba, an angel from Frederick's in Nordstrom
cleaning crew disguise, who created a joyful sanctuary
in the Ladies' Lounge when I needed it most.*

CONTENTS

Acknowledgments   6

Introduction   7

1.   Outside, Inside, All around the Town   11

2.   Movers and Shakers, Associates, and Guests   39

3.   Events, Occasions, and Special Treats   69

4.   Christmas and the One True Santa   97

ACKNOWLEDGMENTS

When Frederick & Nelson (F&N) closed its doors in 1992, Seattle's Museum of History and Industry (MOHAI) became the lucky recipient of more than 46 boxes of materials from the store, including photographs, original artwork, and in-store materials from over 100 years of the store's existence. I would especially like to thank Carolyn Marr, the librarian at MOHAI, for help in navigating this treasure trove. Another great inspiration to me was Robert Spector's wonderful book *More Than a Store: Frederick & Nelson, 1890 to 1990*, commissioned for the store's 100th anniversary. Several Web sites include both personal and public history of F&N, including HistoryLink.org and PDXHistory.com. Thanks to my network of friends, colleagues, and acquaintances that spread the word far and wide that I was seeking F&N pictures and memories to great response. In particular, I'd like to thank the members of RHS75 yahoo group, classmates in MOHAI's Nearby History class, Kimberly Carsberg, and the Dauenhauer, Murray, Allyn, and White families. I also wish to thank Julie Pheasant-Albright, good friend and editor, for suggesting this project and for skipping work with me to attend the final F&N auction. Most of all, I want to acknowledge my parents, Ted and Virginia Wendell, who met in Chicago at Marshall Field & Company and moved here in 1947 for my father's new job in the employment department at Frederick & Nelson, where he remained for 35 years. Their loving preservation of F&N memorabilia has been a legacy enjoyed by my sister, Robin Glover, and me, and has now stood as the basis for this book.

Unless otherwise noted, all images belong to the author's family's personal collection.

Unless otherwise noted, all customer/associate quotes are from memories submitted to Frederick & Nelson during the 1986 Christmas ad campaign; original letters are part of MOHAI's Frederick & Nelson collection.

INTRODUCTION

Frederick & Nelson was founded in Seattle in 1890 by two partners, D. E. Frederick and James Mecham. The two men had worked together in the mines of Colorado and connected again soon after Frederick arrived in Seattle via steamer. They pooled their resources to form a secondhand furniture store they called J. G. Mecham and Company. Soon after, another friend from their mining days arrived from Colorado, Nels Nelson, who purchased a third of the business with cash in hand. Several months later, in ill health, James Mecham sold his share of the business, and the two remaining partners renamed the store Frederick & Nelson. D. E. Frederick had a talent for merchandising and a dedication to providing exemplary service. Nels Nelson's outgoing personality was responsible for forging partnerships and building goodwill in the growing Seattle community. This proved a winning combination, and the partners went on to make good on their vow to create the largest and finest store west of the Mississippi and north of San Francisco.

In 1891, they purchased the Queen City Furniture Company and added new furniture to their inventory. The partners proclaimed, "What our customers want, we will give them. Service is our motto." Early customers included the local Chinook Indians and a city excited by the news that Seattle would soon become the western terminus for the Great Northern Railroad. In 1897, the Klondike Gold Rush pulled Seattle out of the Panic of 1893, and Frederick & Nelson did a brisk business in fine furnishings, supplying both the hotels that catered to the Alaska trade and the homes of what would become the carriage trade.

After several moves, they settled into part of the Rialto Building at Second Avenue and Madison Street. By the early 1900s, Frederick & Nelson operated 28 shiny, horse-drawn delivery wagons. The delivery carriages soon became automobiles and, the oft-told story goes, would bring any purchase to your home from a room full of furniture to a single spool of thread. They instituted a mail-order system with the installation of a telephone switchboard, and if a desired item were not in their shop, they would buy it from some other store. Following on their customer-centric motto was their idea that, "if a customer asks for it, get it, and if enough people want the same thing, start a department." Soon there were departments for furniture, carpeting, housewares, china, and draperies—even a mattress factory.

In 1903, the pair hired Eva MacCallum to open a tearoom. It soon became one of the city's most popular attractions and employed 40 waitresses, a page boy, and a woman dressed as a French maid who sold pastries at each table. By 1906, F&N took up the entire block, including space in other buildings, which were connected by overhead walkways. This same year the store displayed ready-to-wear women's suits and gowns in a corner window, and this was an instant success.

Tragedy struck in 1907. In poor health, Nels Nelson ventured to a medical spa in Bohemia and died at sea upon his return trip. Frederick was left to run the business on his own. By 1914, D. E. Frederick was searching for a single location where he could consolidate all of his merchandise and services. He decided to move six blocks north of Seattle's retail core to Pine Street between Fifth and Sixth Avenues. There he built a six-story building, occupying almost the entire city block, which opened the day after Labor Day on September 3, 1918. More than 25,000 shoppers and guests crossed the threshold of the new store that day.

Businessmen and financiers branded the project "Frederick's Folly" because it was so far away from the established retail area. But Frederick was forward thinking, making sure the foundation was strong enough to hold the 10 stories he felt the store would eventually need. Originally, the building included a beauty salon, post office, an auditorium for showing motion pictures, a fully equipped medical facility, and a nursery. A men-only entrance on the fifth floor spared gentlemen the embarrassment of having to walk through the women's departments. There were reading and writing rooms, and the new, elaborately furnished Tea Room could seat 400. Here fashion shows were held for the enjoyment of the shoppers while they had lunch. Many finished their meal with a Frango, a frozen dessert with a flaky consistency that came in two flavors: maple and orange.

In 1921, the store opened a candy kitchen under the direction of candy maker Ray Alden. Around 1929 it was decided to add a chocolate mint truffle to the line of hard candies and dipped chocolates being produced. Alden's secret recipe included chocolate from cocoa beans grown on the African coast and South America, triple-distilled oil of Oregon Peppermint, and 40 percent butter. The mints became a huge success, in part due to heavy promotion from Gil Ridean, head of F&N's Food Division. They were packaged in a green-and-white eight-ounce tin and were priced at 50¢ a tin. Frango mints became the quintessential Seattle treat.

The store eventually grew to fill those 10 floors and became a center of cultural and civic activity in the Northwest. Besides being the preeminent department store with a rich and varied inventory of merchandise, the store garnered a reputation for hosting all manner of meetings, lectures, and classes, and showcasing local artists, and during World War II, it became the unofficial center for war bond drives.

At the age of 69, D. E. Frederick decided to retire. He had long been impressed with Marshall Field & Company and had patterned many of F&N's policies after the venerable Chicago store. In 1929, he sold Frederick & Nelson to Marshall Field & Company for $6 million. Marshall Field's signed a 99-year lease on the property that would pay Frederick, and later his estate, $100,000 a year. After the sale, Gil Ridean and the candy factory staff went to Chicago to introduce the mints to Marshall Field's executives. Soon they began producing their own version, and the candies began selling all over the country. Frederick & Nelson was the distributor west of the Mississippi, and Marshall Field & Company covered the rest of the nation.

At the time of the sale, William H. St. Clair, who had been merchandise manager, was named president and general manager. He was known, and described in an issue of the staff newsletter, *Between Ourselves*, as a "kindly, quiet man, who manages the store with a firm, friendly hand like the father of an enormous family." In January 1938, Marshall Field's executive William S. Street arrived to fill the number two slot at Frederick & Nelson and was named president in December 1945. Street, and the staff he brought in, led the way in guiding the store through its recovery from the Great Depression, the challenges of World War II, the postwar economic boom, and the store's expansion and changes during the 1950s. One of Street's most influential hires was that of his long-time friend Hector Escobosa to be the person in charge of the fashion direction of the store. Escobosa was widely regarded as a fashion genius and was the first to bring European fashions to Frederick & Nelson. He was also responsible for the development of F&N's specialty departments, such as the gift shop, old world shop, and the 18th-century furniture gallery.

During the 1940s, Frederick & Nelson supported the war efforts in a number of ways and then experienced growth in the expansive years following the war. In 1943, it opened a satellite store at Boeing Field at the Boeing Airplane Company's No. 2 plant. This provided shift workers, many of whom were women, with a convenient place to shop and built loyalty among Boeing's 47,000 employees. F&N also established a Victory Post on the main floor of the Seattle store, selling war bonds and stamps. After the war, Americans began moving to the suburbs, and on August 20, 1946, Bellevue Square opened in downtown Bellevue, becoming the first regional suburban shopping center in the Pacific Northwest. F&N opened its first major branch in Bellevue Square in 1946.

Although the store already had a reputation for its elaborate and stunning holiday displays, it was not until 1943 that Joe Sjursen, director of design, suggested putting Santa Claus himself on display in the Sixth Avenue and Pine Street window. Local children flocked to have a chance to tell Santa what they wanted for Christmas. Art French, the chief photographer for the *Seattle Post-Intelligencer*, is the one credited with coming up with the idea of having children photographed while sitting on Santa's knee. This quickly became a beloved Frederick & Nelson tradition.

In 1952, D. E. Frederick's dreams for expansion of the original store at Pine Street and Fifth Avenue were finally realized when the renovations, spurred by competition from the suburban shopping centers, were finished, and the grand opening was celebrated on August 4, 1952. There were 10 floors and 12 shopping levels (two below ground) built under the guidance of John Graham Jr., son of the original building's architect. On the 10th floor, the company built a modern candy kitchen that could turn out more than 500,000 pounds of Frango mints a year.

The expansion of Frederick & Nelson ignited growth among local retailers and in the core downtown area of Seattle. In a few years, William Street and other local downtown businessmen founded the Seattle Central Association (later named the Downtown Seattle Association) to encourage and maintain the vibrant area. Seattle's present-day exciting and beautiful downtown shopping area can be traced to the vision held by the founders and management of F&N and their decision to expand the store.

In 1955, F&N launched one of the largest retail events ever staged with the $1 million "Sale of Sales." The event was held in what was the largest single room in Seattle—the Field Artillery Armory Drill Hall—where the store offered at least 25 percent off every regularly carried item in the store. Cornelius Byrne, vice president and general manager of the store, was quoted in the *Seattle Post-Intelligencer* as saying, "We set out to put on a warehouse sale . . . aimed directly at young married people who had a great need for household goods at prices they could afford—but who wanted quality as well." The sale garnered national attention with articles in national trade publications and general interest publications as well.

William Street believed, as had D. E. Frederick before him, that a beautiful store with all the amenities, as well as innovations in sales and merchandising, were ultimately not going to be the most important elements in winning the hearts and pocketbooks of their customers. The essential element would be exemplary customer service. When talking of the archetypal customer during a speech to staff he said, "She grades us for honesty—in our merchandise and our advertising. She grades us on our reliability and integrity. How we stand behind our goods. How she can depend on what we tell her. How we keep our promises. She grades us on our courtesy. How pleasant and accommodating we are. How friendly the store is. She grades us on our efficiency. How we do things right the first time . . . The customer . . . who can make or break this business, will continue to decide for us in the future as she has in the past. We stay in business only at the pleasure of the public that purchases our goods and services . . . Remember, We can't get unless we give."

The stories of Frederick & Nelson's customer service became legend throughout the Northwest, and even around the world, for going well beyond the call of duty. A couple of stories in particular have come to embody the qualities for which F&N was known. On December 11, 1927, the "Christmas Ship," bound for Alaska out of Seattle with 107 passengers and a cargo of gifts, was swept onto the rocks during a blinding snowstorm. The passengers were saved, but the entire cargo was ruined. When word reached the store, extra help was hired immediately. All Alaska orders were looked up through thousands of sales slips, and every order was duplicated. Crews worked day and night to get the gifts to the relief ship. Upon docking in Alaska, F&N ensured that, by any means possible, including specially hired airplanes and dog sleds, the gifts were delivered by Christmas.

Katheryn Kavanaugh took a trip to her birthplace in Ireland, a place she had not seen in 20 years. While there, she shot several rolls of color photographs memorializing her trip, and upon her return, she took the film to Frederick & Nelson for processing. The film processor was on the East Coast, and somehow, in the rush of the holiday season, the film was lost in the mail. William Street became involved, meeting with Kavanaugh and asking her to describe the photographs in detail. He then cabled the list to the London office of Marshall Field's, who hired a local photographer, Joseph Hollander, to retrace Katheryn Kavanaugh's route through Ireland

and recreate all the photographs she had taken. Street's proud explanation was, "That is what it takes to create character in a department store."

William Street announced his early retirement in 1961 but continued on as a civic leader. He became chairman of the Century 21 Corporation, the organizing group for the 1962 World's Fair. Frederick's display department put together a series of rotating exhibitions throughout the fairgrounds. Many of the guides wore uniforms chosen by F&N buyers. During the entire run of the fair, the exterior of the store was lit by floodlights, and all the window displays remained lit at night. Inside new carpets were laid, and departments featured products from around the world.

During the 1960s, the world experienced considerable turmoil, and the retail industry and the Northwest itself were not immune. Frederick & Nelson continued on its stately pace, slowed in part by its parent store, Marshall Field & Company. In 1963, F&N opened a $6 million store in Aurora Village Shopping Center, but many felt it was not the size it could have been. In 1968, F&N was included in the Southcenter Mall, but it was felt other retailers gained better location placement. Frederick's survived the depressed economy of Seattle in the 1970s due in large part to their loyal, but aging, customer base. Then in 1978, huge changes came to Marshall Field & Company, and Frederick & Nelson was seen as their best opportunity for growth in a battle waged with their competition, Carter Hawley Hale. By 1980, F&N had become one of the fastest growing stores in the nation, quadrupling from 4 stores to 15. Marshal Field had acquired three Liberty House Stores in Portland and two in Tacoma, as well as six Lipmans stores in Oregon.

The new management, led by G. Arthur Henkens, made changes to the store to try and appeal to the generation of 18–35 year olds, a group who were coming into consumer prominence and with which the store had lost favor. Henkens replaced the bargain basement with the Arcade, a public marketplace-styled collection of food, candy, coffee, and trendy new housewares like espresso machines and pasta makers, and added a junior apparel boutique called "Pzaz." But these changes, undertaken within a poor business climate, spelled the beginning of the end for Frederick's. Throughout the 1980s, F&N was passed around to various investors like the unwanted fruitcake at Christmas, losing money at every turn. There was a moment of hope in 1986 when the store came under local ownership again. That Christmas the store ran a campaign with the tag line: "It was Frederick & Nelson then. Now it's Frederick & Nelson again." They asked customers to send in letters about their own F&N memories and received more than 2,500 responses. Clearly, the people of Seattle, and beyond, still cherished the memory of what the store had been. But the memories and goodwill were not enough to keep the store afloat, and after one last valiant effort in 1989 by local businessman David Sabey to turn things around, the magnificent old store slipped away in 1992. Gone but not forgotten, these images celebrate the glory days of a great American department store: Frederick & Nelson.

One

OUTSIDE, INSIDE, ALL AROUND THE TOWN

Prompted by news of the Great Northern Railroad choosing Seattle for its western terminus, the population of Seattle exploded, as did its economy. Frederick & Nelson followed suit. D. E. Frederick and Nels Nelson, pictured here at far left (from left to right), moved their store several times in the early days, but by 1892, it was settled into this space at 208–210 Pike Street.

With the 1891 acquisition of the Queen City Furniture Company, Frederick & Nelson added the sale of new furniture. This was prompted in part by the increase in competition, which had made secondhand furniture scarce but still in high demand. One night, when Nelson returned to the room he shared with Frederick (pictured center above), he found the bed missing—sold to one of their customers.

On a snowy Christmas Eve in 1890, a customer wanted to purchase a secondhand rocker for his wife for Christmas but only if it could be delivered that night. The partners climbed to the top of Denny Hill, trading off carrying the heavy chair on their backs. This was the first delivery in the history of F&N.

Frederick & Nelson purchased the assets of the Pacific Carpet Company in 1897 and then consolidated with Silas Munro's New England Furniture Store. At this point, the name changed again, to Frederick, Nelson, and Munro. Munro, however, was apprehensive of expanding too rapidly and soon parted company with Frederick & Nelson.

Their second move in 1897 took the store to the Rialto Building on Second Avenue and Madison Street, where they leased two floors. They installed an elevator, which was one of the first in the city and became an attraction for both locals and out-of-towners. With their expanded line of merchandise, the store was rapidly becoming a department store.

Construction on the new store on Pine Street between Fifth and Sixth Avenues began in 1916. It took two years to complete due to the shortage of materials caused by World War I. Thirty thousand square feet of pink marble covered the first floor, and the building itself was built of reinforced concrete finished with terra-cotta.

Frederick & Nelson employees pitched in to complete the work needed on the new building by laying carpets, building furnishings, and decorating. On Labor Day weekend in 1918, F&N's 1,230 employees moved every piece of merchandise into the new building, with each department manager riding in the truck that carried his stock. This photograph commemorates this Herculean task.

Erecting the new store on Pine Street was referred to by many as "Frederick's Folly" because the location was considered out of town. In this 1918 photograph, the neighborhood is still residential, but this did not last for long. After Frederick & Nelson's moved to Pine Street, the rest of Seattle's department stores soon made the move to that area of town as well, which remains the heart of Seattle's retail district.

In 1929, the year of this photograph, D. E. Frederick sold Frederick & Nelson to Marshall Field & Company for $6 million. Field's signed a lease for the property that would pay Frederick and his heirs $100,000 a year for 99 years. The building remained in Frederick's family until 1996 when they sold it to Nordstrom.

A seven-story service building and warehouse was built on Terry Avenue in 1928, a few blocks from F&N. It was needed to handle the overflow of goods and services from the main store and included workrooms and fur storage vaults. In this photograph, Frederick's impressive fleet of delivery vehicles can be seen lined up outside.

F&N opened the Cottage Shop on Boeing Airplane Company's grounds in 1943 so that thousands of defense workers could shop between shifts and on lunch hours. The store carried such items as full lines of work clothing, street suits, slacks, blouses, toiletries, lingerie, candy, cosmetics, and hosiery. Cutting down on deliveries conserved gasoline, oil, and rubber on the truck tires.

In 1940, the Lacey V. Murrow Bridge opened up the east side of Lake Washington for suburban expansion. Frederick & Nelson's first suburban store followed in 1946 in the Bellevue Shopping Square. Although enlarged from the 20,000 square feet originally planned, it was still too small, and in 1956, a new 116,000-square-foot store replaced it. This photograph shows the original 1946 building.

The Bellevue Store opened its doors on August 20, 1946 to crowds that packed the sidewalks before the 1:00 p.m. opening hour. Civic leaders of Bellevue and other towns on the east side were present for a radio broadcast, as were Frederick & Nelson executives and staff. With the main store and Bellevue store, a service building, two warehouses, and the candy factory, the F&N "empire" now totaled six buildings.

Starting in 1949, a remodel occurred that took three years to build the store from 5.5 stories to 10. This was one of the first major department store expansions in any metropolitan city in the United States. Over the next three years following the remodel, there were more than 30 major improvements and expansions in downtown Seattle. F&N president William Street stated, "Frederick's gave courage to others."

In August 1952, *Town and Country* put out a special "Greater Frederick & Nelson Edition" to highlight the store's new look. This lovely Edward Hopper–like photograph was included. The caption read in part, "It is not often that you can actually see a 'belief' . . . but you do, in the photograph above. This big, beautiful, newly expanded Frederick & Nelson is a visual, practical expression of the store's confidence in Seattle's future."

The Crescent, a department store in Spokane, joined Frederick & Nelson in being part of the Marshall Field's family with the merger of the Spokane Dry Goods Company and Marshall Field's in June 1969. This was seen as an opportunity to expand into the inland empire of the Northwest.

Cornelius Byrne succeeded William Street as president and managed F&N through the 1960s. He did not have the in with the Marshall Field's staff that Street had, Street having been one of them, and expansion plans he made were reined in by the parent company. The Aurora Village store opened in 1963 but was only 154,000 square feet. Here the Seattle Thunderbirds, a drum and bugle corps, perform at the opening.

When the Southcenter Mall was planned, other local retailers, such as the Bon Marché, J. C. Penney, and Nordstrom-Best, staked their claims on sites a year ahead of Frederick's, who ended up in a wing that was added on later. Completed in 1968, the Southcenter store would be Frederick & Nelson's last significant new real estate venture for 10 years.

Frederick & Nelson expanded south to the Tacoma Mall in 1978, the same year 32-year-old G. Arthur Henkens was brought in by Marshall Field's to be president and CEO. He had begun his career as a part-time associate at Frederick's while in high school in Bellevue and had held the positions of general merchandise manager and executive vice president at Meier and Frank in Portland.

In the fall of 1989, under David Sabey's leadership, F&N opened its first new store in eight years—a $3.7 million, 120,000-square-foot store in south Tacoma's Lakewood Mall. Sabey also spent $3 million remodeling the flagship store's main floor, its first modernization in almost 40 years. Sabey had been inundated with suggestions from longtime F&N customers on how to bring back Frederick's to its old standards . . . including his mother!

This window display dates from the time of the Alaska-Yukon-Pacific Exposition in 1909. For a fashionable lady of the time, an ostrich-plumed hat like those shown was de rigueur. F&N was among the civic leaders promoting the exposition. When sale of stock for the exposition opened, F&N ran an advertisement titled "Everybody Helps." The subscription reached $600,000 on the second day, and the exposition put Seattle in the spotlight.

Ready-to-wear was a new concept in the early 1900s, as all fine clothes had until then been made to order. In September 1906, with little fanfare, a display of women's ready-to-wear appeared in a corner window of F&N. By the second day of the display, F&N added thanks to its feminine readers in a newspaper advertisement for the "warm welcome accorded the costume and suit section."

When World War II ended, retailing began to boom as Americans were only too happy to throw off shortages and rationing, and begin buying again. In the first month postwar, August 1945, F&N reinstituted fashion shows in the Tea Room, and window displays reflected flights of fancy, such as these ladies in swimsuits cavorting with giant sea horses.

Chester Bowles, U.S. president Franklin D. Roosevelt's price administrator, praised department stores such as Frederick & Nelson for their bond-selling campaigns. He stated, "More than 70 million Americans have found that the war bonds sold in department stores have been a convenient way to invest their excess purchasing power." After the war ended, Americans' thoughts turned to other purchases, and Studebakers replaced Jeeps in the store's windows.

In 1949, Bon Marché's parent company, Allied Stores, announced it would be building the first major shopping mall in the country in Seattle's Northgate area. Marshall Field's refused to be a part of a project owned by a competitor but did agree to expand the downtown store. This window display detailed the expansion and modernization plans.

After the remodeled store opened in August 1952, women's wear merchandising manager Richard Bond chartered airplanes to fly in the store's top apparel manufacturers from California and New York. These beautifully lit windows along Pine Street highlighted all the quality and stylishness of the apparel offered in the renewed store.

Christmas window displays of television sets drew big crowds in 1949. The year before, thousands of people had crowded into Frederick & Nelson to see the first local television broadcast by KRSC, Seattle's only television station at the time.

In this 1967 image from the Don Sherwood Parks History Collection is an example of some of the innovative displays for which Frederick & Nelson was known. Here the mannequins are posed in front of a replica of the Volunteer Park Conservatory, and live plants are landscaped all around them. (Courtesy Seattle Municipal Archives, No. 30998.)

In another image from the Don Sherwood Parks History Collection, a classic Northwest outdoor scene shows a Frederick & Nelson display signature—the use of live animals in window displays. This representation of the Children's Zoo at Seattle's Woodlawn Park was complete with miniature goats trotting around, nibbling on the scenery. (Courtesy Seattle Municipal Archives, No. 30995.)

Continuing the parks department theme, this display window shows a Northwest family preparing to sit down at a picnic table for a meal. The set is landscaped to include several pine trees, giving the impression of camping in a local forest. It is easy to imagine that the family may have visited the Eddie Bauer Sports Shop, featuring outdoor equipment, before their trip. (Courtesy Seattle Municipal Archives, No. 30996.)

Here again is the use of live animals—in this case, birds—in an enclosure within the landscaped display. Hopefully, this display was not meant to appeal to those customers who frequented the target range in the basement of the store's sports shop. (Courtesy Seattle Municipal Archives, No. 30997.)

This advertisement in the special edition of *Town and Country*, while clearly getting across the message that Frederick & Nelson is "first in fashion," still manages to show Frederick's understated style. Advertising director Reginald Morgan was quoted in a 1921 article in *Women's Wear Daily* as saying, "Frederick & Nelson considers that the capital crime in advertising is to 'over-advertise' . . . [which is] an undue enthusiasm expressed in print, and in which our customers may decline to concur upon actual inspection of our offerings."

Fashion was not just for women at Frederick & Nelson; the store also enjoyed a reputation as a leading haberdashery. A custom shop offered suits made to measure, and men's furnishings, sportswear, and hat and shoe shops, completing head-to-toe coverage. The men's areas were located away from the usual shopping traffic, and the decor was "masculine and substantial" to complete the sense of being in a "man's world."

Anita McAtee, merchandise manager of women's apparel during the 1950s, said, "We built our fashion reputation by working closely with the designers and heads of companies. . . . No one has to buy anything, but when you make the merchandise appealing and exciting, success comes." Merchandisers teamed with the award-winning advertising and display departments to coordinate each season's fashion campaign.

Local manufacturers and suppliers were just as important to Frederick & Nelson as international designers. The store held a breakfast each year recognizing such local companies as Pacific Trail Sportswear, pictured in this advertisement. William Street said that these companies "were important to the community and to ourselves. We were going to nurture them."

Equally important to Frederick & Nelson's presence in national publications was the impression it made in the local media. This advertisement in the April 4, 1966, issue of the *Seattle Shopping News* for imported French kid gloves directs shoppers to the budget floor and emphasizes their "excellent value."

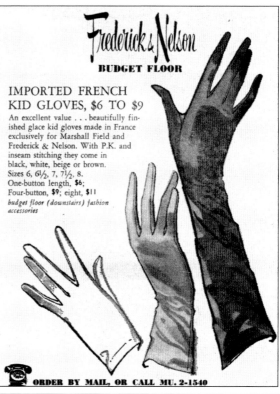

Frederick & Nelson
BUDGET FLOOR

IMPORTED FRENCH
KID GLOVES, $6 TO $9

An excellent value . . . beautifully finished glace kid gloves made in France exclusively for Marshall Field and Frederick & Nelson. With P.K. and inseam stitching they come in black, white, beige or brown. Sizes 6, 6½, 7, 7½, 8. One-button length, **$6**; Four-button, **$9**; eight, **$11** *budget floor (downstairs) fashion accessories*

ORDER BY MAIL, OR CALL MU. 2-1540

A CORNER OF THE FURNITURE GALLERIES, FREDERICK AND NELSON, SEATTLE, WASH.

In the early 1900s, furniture was sold from stores that might be stuffed to the rafters or have all different types of furniture mixed together. A customer might glimpse a chair she thought she wanted hanging from the ceiling, but when it was taken down, it was not at all what she had in mind. Frederick's furniture galleries, where customers could walk around the furniture and see pieces arranged as they would be used, were unique.

When William Street arrived at F&N in 1938, he faced a city still caught up in a Depression economy and a store that was flagging. One of his first acts was to bring in his friend Hector Escobosa as executive in charge of fashion. Anita McAtee said of him, "He instilled in everyone the idea . . . that the world was ours to buy from." Shown above is a designer showroom around 1939.

Hector Escobosa's influence went beyond couture, and by the early 1940s, Frederick & Nelson's had gained a reputation for its name-brand home furnishings, such as Wedgewood China and Karastan rugs, as well as its specialty departments. These specialty shops included the old world shop and the rarity shop (pictured above), which featured antique furniture, silver, and glassware.

Here is the entrance to the men's shop, shown around 1944, which blanketed the Pine Street side of the store on the main floor. During this time, it had a special section for uniforms of the nation's armed forces.

As with other departments, the toy section glowed with postwar vigor in the late 1940s and early 1950s. Located in the youth center on the fifth floor, it was busy all year-round. Sales associate Marilyn Fike recalls "one lady brought back a toy truck that appeared to have been run over by a *real* truck. She said it fell apart. We took it back, of course."

After the remodel of the early 1950s, the youth shops moved to the fourth floor, where *Town and Country* described them as "bright with young fashions for every age, from carriage to high school." Also on this floor was a special lounge where mothers could care for their babies. Shown here is the infant department, from which many a Seattle baby received their layette.

The Steuben Glass Room opened to the public on June 23, 1952 following a week-long preview that included a reception for the press. The elegant room was designed expressly to display a complete selection of famous Steuben crystal. For a limited time, there were engraved pieces from private and public collections on display as well. Emily Laighton, formerly with Steuben's Fifth Avenue shop in New York, was the manager.

The March/April 1961 edition of *Between Ourselves* announced "an event of exceptional interest to every staff member"—the selling of antique furnishings from the estate of D. E. Frederick. The event took place in Exhibition Hall, with an invitational preview at night. Most pieces were of museum significance and had been collected during Frederick's lifetime from all over the world.

F&N was an active participant in the 1962 World's Fair. Above is an exhibit of the U.S. Rubber Company that was designed and created by Blanche Morgan (pictured) of the Studio of Interior Design at F&N. It is called "Higashi Nishi," meaning East and West, and incorporated both living and garden areas with a blend of Far Eastern and Western design elements.

While the main store was renowned for its spectacular displays and abundance of quality merchandise, this photograph shows that the suburban stores were also havens of elegance. Here is the silver and gift departments of the Bellevue Square store after a remodel in 1979. The departments were relocated to the second level, adjacent to china.

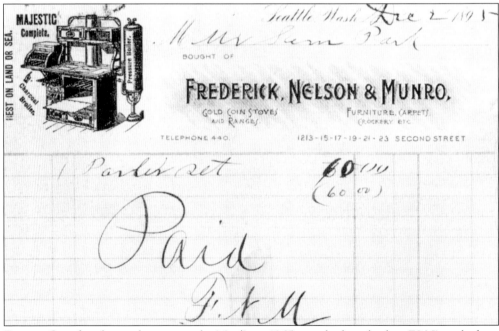

Between Ourselves featured a story in the May/June 1965 issue looking back at F&N's early days. Lillian Park, an associate in the mail shopping service, brought in the 1895 statement shown above. In the 1986 memories campaign, customer Harriet Stigenwalt related having a sales slip from 1894 that showed the $8.85 her parents (her father a Norwegian immigrant) paid for the housewares they purchased to set up housekeeping.

The finest of the delivery teams was "Bess and Bell," dapple grays that took all the cups at the horse shows, including the coveted trophies from Victoria, British Columbia. They were driven by William Edward Jones. The mares grew to be as famous as Frederick & Nelson itself and were seen as a symbol of the store until their retirement to an idyllic pasture.

As more and more streets became paved, motor trucks were introduced into the fleet. The old horse-and-wagon teams were relegated to any long haul trips on the remaining unpaved, often muddy, Seattle roads. This photograph from the early 1900s shows the team in what looks to be a prosperous residential neighborhood with large houses but still unpaved streets.

Here the entire fleet is lined up and awaiting their delivery assignments. Every morning when the store opened, the teams assembled and were driven in tight formation down Second Avenue from their stables to the Madison Street Service Building. Passersby stopped and watched in admiration of the beautiful horses. Block and tackle was used to keep the teams from falling on the steep hill, and blocks and ropes supplemented this in icy weather.

The partners started to see automobiles coming into use but felt them inadequate for the steep hills and muddy roads of Seattle. They did, however, buy cars for personal use to "try them out" and were finally convinced that trucks could be practical. Pictured above is the F&N fleet of trucks that did not have license plates issued but had big numbers painted on them as identification.

The smiling delivery man in this 1944 photograph may well have just risen from the subbasement of the store in the delivery service's own private elevator on the west end of the concourse. Trucks brought goods to the receiving room and loaded packages from the packing room to deliver to the delivery department in the service building. Another truck elevator at the east end of the concourse lifted trucks to the fourth and fifth floor levels.

During the flood of 1933, F&N vans continued to make deliveries. When trucks could go no farther, packages were transferred to rowboats so deliveries could be completed. Every package reached its destination. Here John "Pat" Brennan is seen delivering holiday packages to the Anderson family of Hoquiam, Washington.

Here the men of the delivery team pose in their starched white coats next to their shiny service vans with sleek 1950s styling. June Jensen Allen remembered a time years before this in 1937 when she had the opportunity to ride in the delivery truck. She worked in the alterations department and rode along to Broadmoor, an exclusive gated community, to attend to a bride and her attendants, assuring that their altered gowns were exactly right.

For F&N's 75th anniversary, the delivery department got a new look. Pictured here from left to right are (first row) Donald Anderson, John Vagovic, Reginald James, George Buckley, Joe Morris, Dave Andrews, Stanley Mitzrak, Carl Horne, Thomas Davis, Maurice Simpson, Robert Gwinn, Arthur Lorrain, and Raymond Johnson; (second row) Dick Casebere, Karl Victor, Howard Staup, Ray Ledwich, Robert Dorgan, John Kelly, Lloyd LaPlante, Allen Wolfe, Oscar Lundstrom, Thomas Peterson, Damian Flynn, Keith White, John Hackel, Loren Loesell, Les Albright, Maurice Christopherson, Frank Noble, and George Ellis (manager, wearing suit).

Two

MOVERS AND SHAKERS, ASSOCIATES, AND GUESTS

James Mecham, Frederick & Nelson's original business partner, said that Frederick (left) was "endowed by the Creator with an unusually brilliant mind, and with an unswerving purpose and moral courage to do, at all times, the right as he saw it. He was a bundle of dynamic energy, and every hair of his red head radiated energy to those about him." Nelson (right), he said, was "truly one of God's noblemen."

S. H. Clement was Frederick & Nelson's first staff member. He was photographed here during a visit to the store in the late 1940s. He was hired in 1891 when F&N was just one year old and attended the Golden Anniversary Banquet for staff members in 1940.

In December 1945, it was announced that William Street had decided to return to F&N, having completed his most pressing duties at the Chicago store. He was appointed president to replace Charles Bunker, who was retiring. He was welcomed home at a breakfast given for him in the Tea Room on January 16, 1946, an event which was attended by more than 250 executives, department heads, and buyers.

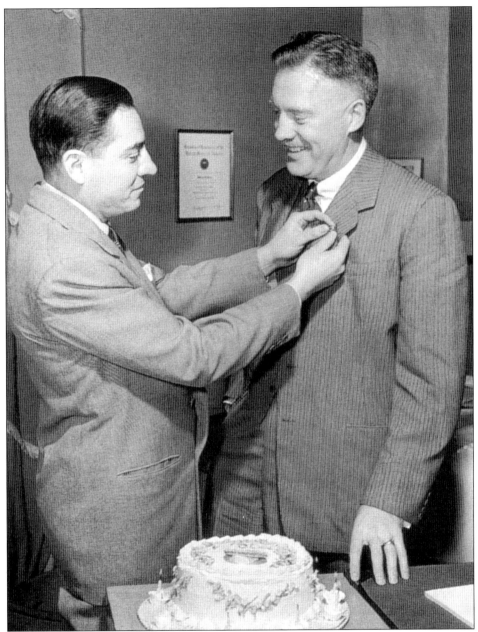

General manager Hector Escobosa (left) was thrilled to have his friend and colleague William Street (right) return to the store. Street had a few regrets about leaving Chicago but had told the Marshall Field staff: "We believe in the future of Seattle. Whatever contribution we can make in business or community activities we intend to make it—and we'll get a kick out of doing it." Soon after Street's return, F&N played host to 36 of the nation's top fashion designers, heralding the return of fashionable merchandise to the city. In May 1946, Escobosa made the first buying trip abroad since before the war. Frederick & Nelson soon became the city's headquarters for imported merchandise, including European designer originals and couture collections. Escobosa said, "We believe we will grow as the Pacific Northwest grows, that we have a responsibility to this region, and that the future has no limit but our foresight and courage."

In June 1949, at the first board meeting in Seattle, members of the Marshall Field & Company board of directors discuss Frederick & Nelson's expansion plans. From left to right are James L. Palmer, John P. Wilson, Hector Escobosa, Marshall Field III, William Street, Hughston M. McBain, Albert B. Dick Jr., Henry P. Isham, and Stanley Field.

Seattle's David Sabey bought F&N in 1989 and attempted a comeback. In the *Seattle Post-Intelligencer* in November 1996 he said, "But for a few more dollars and a little bit of support, Frederick's would be alive and well today. Isn't it ironic that today we could find $20–$30 million extra for a parking garage, but five years ago we couldn't find 10¢ to save a wonderful part of Seattle's history?"

Your Career at Frederick & Nelson and its predecessor, *Frederick Nelson and You,* bear little resemblance to the dry pedantic employee manuals encountered today. Filled with pictures and inspiring stories of the founders' vision, as well as detailed explanations of the many employee "perks," it is easy to see why those who worked at the store were often envied. This illustration is from the front cover of the publication in the late 1950s or early 1960s.

It was said if all the records of all the staff members that were handled by personnel were laid end to end, they would reach to outer space and back. Holding employee entry forms from left to right are manager Ted Wendell, Florence Mack, Jacqueline Clark, Betty Lou Woodbridge, Dorothy Cuff, Letha Parks, Earlene Lockwood, and assistant manager Estella Hawes.

The annual ship-shape campaign was designed as a store spring cleaning. George Gunn (kneeling), prime minister to the 1st Lord of the Admiralty Joe Cooper (being measured), measures the officers of the H. M. S. Frederick & Nelson for their official uniforms. Looking on are (from left to right) Jack Hupf, 3rd Lord of the Admiralty; Frank Peabody, 2nd Lord of the Admiralty; and Curt Larson of the sign shop.

Employees are shown relaxing in the employee roof garden in this June 1952 photograph. The roof garden, for summer use by staff, opened on June 2nd that year with punch and cookies served. Some of the female staff have taken advantage of the summer rules to add the daring addition of white to the accepted dress colors of black, navy blue, dark brown, beige, or gray.

These associates were surely well aware of the store's stand on matters of good taste. As stated in the 1944 *Frederick & Nelson and You*, "If you consider these practices for a moment, you, too, will agree that they are not appropriate in business." These include "participation in popularity contests, beauty competitions, or other publicity promotions, collection of money among staff members for the giving of gifts."

Also frowned upon by management was "participation in football or baseball pools, betting, buying and selling of chances, or other similar enterprises while in the store." Obviously, an exciting game of checkers while enjoying a good cigar was exempt.

Nearly 2,000 staff members participated in the Stech Morale Survey given in 1950 at the Eagle's Auditorium. Introductory talks were given by William Street, Myron Law, and Hector Escobosa. Street had previously commissioned an in-store survey in 1946, whose results showed some negative feelings from staff. In reaction, he instituted human relations training and a service improvement program.

There were recreation activities available for F&N staff in most every sport or leisure activity. Shown here is one of the store's bowling teams, who had "modern alleys located not far from the store." In a 1961 *Between Ourselves*, the news was that the come-from-behind Guttersnipes won the first half of the championship, and the Bocci Boys were in the lead for the second half.

Basketball was also popular over the years at F&N. In 1957, the F&N team ended the first half of the commercial league play in second place. Don Donahou was considered the bulwark of the F&N scoring machine with a 20-plus average per game. Fast forward to 1973, and the boys played hard but could not rise above third place. Above, coach Karl Victor lays out the strategy for the next quarter's play.

The great books class, shown here in 1950, discussed classics on alternate Tuesday evenings in the Tea Room. Members had two weeks to read the selection and two lively hours to discuss it. In 1972, the F&N chapter celebrated its silver anniversary with five of the original members of the group still active participants. Selections for that year included works by Aristotle, Geoffrey Chaucer, Benedictus de Spinoza, Herman Melville, Charles Darwin, Henry James, and others.

Frederick & Nelson and You tempted staff members to the library with promises of "fiction, mystery, travel, and the stories of men's lives." There one could also obtain an emergency sewing kit or writing paper. By 1961, the library (actually the smallest branch of the Seattle Public Library system) had more than 1,000 books and pamphlets. Overdue fines were about to rise from 2¢ a day to 5¢.

The Frederick & Nelson Chorus was a staff group organized for singing carols during the holiday season. Clara Magnussen sent in her memories of singing "many mornings for the enjoyment of customers" during the 1930s. They rehearsed in the Tea Room and were directed by Orville Belstad. Magnussen also remembered being accompanied on the piano by "a very handsome young man—Mr. John Sundsten!" The chorus is pictured here in 1950.

The staff of the employee cafeteria is pictured here in 1959. It was reported that the previous year they had served over half a million snacks and meals. In the 1944 employee manual, the cafeteria was recommended for "good food and moderate prices." Staff members could also use the Fountain Lunch and the Tea Room, but women were reminded to "always wear their wraps."

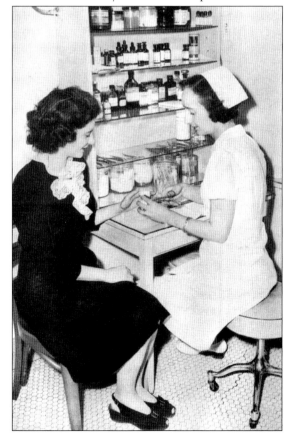

Frederick & Nelson had a complete medical department available to their staff. Nurses were on duty all day, and a doctor and dentist could be consulted three mornings a week. Physical and dental exams could be scheduled, and other services, such as vaccinations, were offered. The medical department also provided first aid to customers in case of an emergency.

In 1946, strikes were happening all over the country, including a particularly bitter one that happened that year in Seattle's newspaper industry. The women's signs in this photograph read, "Signed, Elevator Operators, Janitors, Janitresses." More than 10 years later, in 1959, William Street would give an impassioned speech where he warned against the "penalties to innocent bystanders" strikes can bring. (Courtesy Frederick & Nelson Records, MOHAI, Seattle.)

With sincere appreciation of **20** years' continuous
service as a Frederick & Nelson staff member
the management takes pleasure in presenting to

Ted Wendell

THIS CERTIFICATE, AS A TOKEN OF HIGH REGARD

Frederick & Nelson . . . Seattle
A DIVISION OF MARSHALL FIELD & COMPANY

PRESIDENT

Frederick & Nelson felt that rewarding long service was a sincere reflection of the store's appreciation for the outstanding loyalty of its staff. Each milestone of an associate's career was marked with special presentations, starting with the 10th year and continuing every five years thereafter. Extra vacation time, merchandise, and checks were awarded to staff with long service. The 30 Year Club was a much-honored group that met annually for a special luncheon.

F&N's retirement program was established in 1943 and was one of the first, and remained one of the best, programs in the industry. It included a trusteed pension plan and an insured annuity plan that provided life insurance until retirement and then additional income. This photograph in *Your Career at Frederick & Nelson* illustrated the retirement lifestyle, which most likely did not include wearing a tie while mowing the lawn.

Every issue of *Between Ourselves* included some staff retirement plans. In this photograph from 1952, two beauty salon associates plot their trips. Gertrude Heltsley (left) was to tour the United States for 6 months while Caroline Gallant (right) planned to return to Norway after being away for more than 45 years.

OUR BUSINESS CREED

FREDERICK & NELSON our watchword.
Remember always, courtesy is the keynote
   of our service to the public.
Endeavor each day to become more efficient
Doing a good deed will help in the day's
   work.
Encourage initiative in each salesperson.
Recognize no impediments except we
   master them.
Instill loyalty and respect in our business
   associates.
Carefully make promises and sacredly ful-
   fill them.
Keep our minds and bodies healthy. A good
   housekeeper keeps a clean house.
& Furthermore—
Never let idle gossip influence our own good
   judgment.
Eliminate errors so that there can be no re-
   currence.
Love our work.
Sell goodwill as well as good merchandise.
Organize our mental faculties so that we can
   do the right thing at the right time.
Neglect no detail in our program for better
   buying and better selling.   E. P.

Frederick & Nelson's philosophy of customer care and service was present from the beginning and started at the top with D. E. Frederick's Business Creed. It was later expressed as the Frederick & Nelson Idea and included such basics as "to do the right thing at the right time, in the right way; to do some things better than they were ever done before . . . to be satisfied with nothing short of perfection."

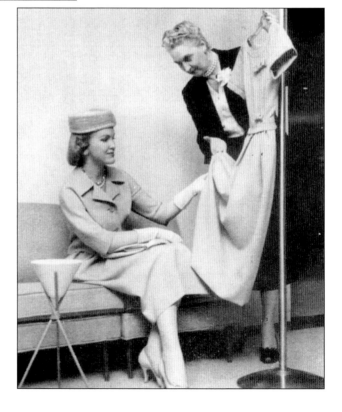

Here designer room associate Hazel Neilsen shows a Dior dress to Jane Anderson. The March/April 1957 issue of *Between Ourselves* reminded associates of the "Seven Selling Statements"—name, use, quality points, benefits, special features, care, and price—and that knowing the right names and how to pronounce them was essential.

This 1904 photograph shows the staff members of the furniture department when Frederick & Nelson was located in the Rialto Building. The particular troubles of the furniture store buyer were covered by H. H. Oothoudt in *Between Ourselves* many years later when he told of traveling from one manufacturer to another, trying to match pieces by memory alone.

The tube room, looking like a giant pipe organ, was located in the subbasement. The containers, which carried customer's cash and sales checks, twisted around from floor to floor inside the tubes and popped out from what *Frederick & Nelson and You* said looked to be "Paul Bunyan's telephone switchboard." Change would be made, and the carriers would be sent back in the same way.

The packing room was also in the subbasement. Steve Camp related to the author his memories of working at Christmas 1958–1960. "My job was rolling those big canvas carts around to the various cash registers on the toy floor, picking up the sold goods, and taking them to the back room where we sent them cascading down chutes to the basement for gift wrapping and mailing or delivery."

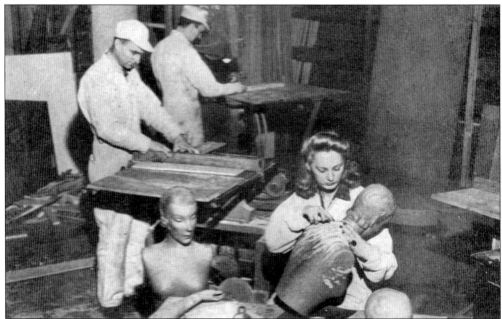

The display shop was located in the service building on Terry Avenue. Here almost all the display pieces used in the store were fabricated or "renewed." The exterior displays, in three blocks of 20 windows, were carefully planned many weeks ahead. Those who worked in the service building were exempt from the dress code, needing only to be "suitably dressed for your work."

In a city that would gain a reputation as the outdoor equipment capital of the world with such retailers as Eddie Bauer and REI, there was a time in the late 1940s when Frederick & Nelson held the distinction of the best sporting goods department in Seattle. Bernie Hall is pictured here, an expert in fishing tackle.

A customer wrote to the store in 1955 stating, "In one department I spent $30.00 and in another 12¢—yet I received the same courteous treatment for both purchases." Pictured here is Marian Beale from the garden shop instructing other associates in sales techniques. They are reminded that "a fine product can be a failure if the salesperson fails to tell the customer how to use it."

Many Seattleites of a certain age remember the Children's Shoes Department as an essential part of their back-to-school buying trip. Whether it was the saddle shoes required by the parochial schools or something a bit snappier, like this girl's patent leather Mary Janes, Frederick's was the place to buy them. A favorite moment was climbing the stairs to the little wooden bridge at the end of the department in new shoes for all to admire. Julie Pheasant-Albright remembers vividly childhood visits to F&N, especially the carousel theme in the Children's Clothing Department dressing room. Each door on the changing rooms had a different decorated horse riding its merry-go-round pole. After she and her brother and sister were outfitted for school, their mother would drop them off in the Kindergarten, where a favorite activity was making necklaces from straws and bits of wrapping paper. With three children within a year of each other in age, their mother was no doubt glad of some time on her own to shop.

Frederick & Nelson's best browsing area was the book department, which offered magazines and book rentals in addition to the large and varied collection of books for sale. On display here is the best seller *Skid Road: An Informal Portrait of Seattle* by Murray Morgan, published in 1951.

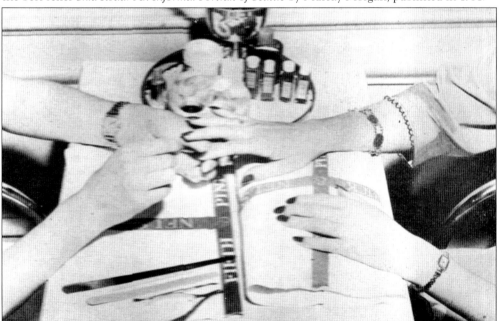

Frederick & Nelson's Beauty Salon, originally referred to as the Temple of Venus, grew to be one of the largest salons in the country. In the 1930s, Frederick's housed the only Elizabeth Arden salon west of Chicago and north of San Francisco. The salon also offered hair styling and treatments. A children's hairdressing salon was added in the remodel, and the author remembers fondly getting her regular "pixie cut."

Pictured above is Austa Proudlock of the notions department, who provided the Frederick & Nelson version of "Heloise's Hints" by finding answers to many of the customers' household problems. Here she is giving a demonstration, imparting tips on how to make upholstery look new and fresh again and ready for spring.

An associate is shown here working in the picture frame workshop located in the service building. There were special workshops for draperies, upholstery, Venetian blinds and shades, and carpets as well. The store also employed a "fix-it man," who was said to be "a wizard at replacing hard-to-find parts, restoring efficiency to practically any household item."

Peggy Hardan wrote that the highlight of her F&N trips as a child was "watching the beautiful elevator operators of course. Smiling, pretty girls dressed in smart uniforms, obeying the commands of their 'starter' . . . cleverly tapping out their instructions on her clicker. What glamour! For years I dreamed that I would grow up to be beautiful enough so one day I could join their elite group!"

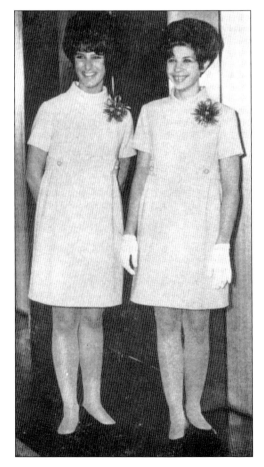

Being an F&N elevator operator was *the* prestige job for a Seattle high school girl. Operators had to be approximately the same size and look, and have short dark hair. In this photograph in the November/December 1968 issue of *Between Ourselves*, Sandra Parnell (left) and Jan Christen (right) show you did not need to be a blonde to have more fun.

To paraphrase a famous F&N slogan, "a wedding isn't a wedding without a day, or many days, at Frederick & Nelson." Over the years, the brides of Seattle would definitely agree. In the 1960s, the bridal shop, run by Sarah Johnson (far right), was central headquarters for the busy bride. Next door was the tip to toe department for apparel, accessories, and lingerie for the bride, wedding party, and mothers of the bride and groom.

Mary Pat Hall wrote of "the most important event of my life—my wedding. My mother and I were going to pick out my wedding dress . . . for such a special occasion it had to be from F&N. We found the 'perfect dress.'" Thirty years later, for her daughter's wedding, Hall said, "We'll take the dress to F&N, they'll know how to restore and alter it." It was again the "perfect dress."

The bride's wedding gown was the most thrilling purchase of all. It could be special ordered in whatever color and fabric the bride chose. When Marjorie Josephine Beede married Raymond Frederick Allyn Sr., pictured here in the foyer of the Sigma Kappa House of the University of Washington on January 31, 1942, she and her bridesmaids all wore dresses from Frederick & Nelson. (Courtesy the Allyn family.)

"The Brides of Spring" was the theme of the 1973 bridal show, which took place in the Restaurant (the abysmal new moniker for the Tea Room that no self-respecting Seattleite ever used). The gowns shown were said to be "indicative of spring '73's trends," which, in true 1970s fashion, were pretty abysmal as well.

The flower shop provided all kinds of bouquets and wedding flowers, from a simple corsage to a "sheaf of orchids." Shown above are Vivian Holmes (left) and Alice Belt (right), who designed each bouquet to a bride's individual taste and ensured a setting in which each bride could shine. A bride could even have her attendants' pumps dyed to match her flower choice.

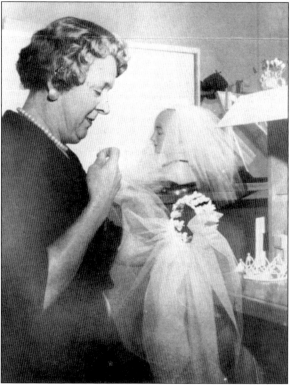

Veils and attendants' hats were handmade in the millinery workroom. Pictured at left is Helen McDermott, putting the final stitches on a bridal veil. Another department brought into play for wedding planning might have been the portrait salon, to capture forever all this finery.

Ilse Samson puts the final flower on this tiered wedding cake from the Frederick & Nelson bakeshop. Every food department could be involved in wedding plans, providing food for engagement parties, rehearsal dinners, and the wedding itself. The Tea Room was a popular venue for engagement luncheons and wedding showers. Parties of up to 500 could be accommodated.

Honeymoon plans could be handled through Frederick & Nelson's Ask Mr. Foster travel service. Pictured are Darlene Huntley (left) and Georgianna Jeklin (right), who helped plan itineraries and secured reservations and tickets, whether it was for a weekend in Victoria, B.C., or a cruise around the world. Sturdy and handsome luggage could, of course, be purchased in the luggage department.

The September/October 1965 *Between Ourselves* posited that the Native American women selling their hand woven baskets in the picture above were the forerunners of the Bellevue Arts and Crafts Fair that was held outside the door of the Bellevue store. Some records indicate that the woman at far left was Princess Angeline, daughter of Chief Sealth. It was said that Princess Angeline was never charged for any store purchases.

Kenneth Rusk has a childhood memory of Mrs. Alfred Anderson (pictured above), last of Seattle's carriage trade, arriving at F&N "to be greeted by a regal doorman." He went on to say, "Impressive as this was, what impressed my young mind most was the way my mother and I were greeted with the same savoir faire even though we arrived on a big lumbering yellow streetcar."

Lewis C. "Clark" Pounds, pictured here in a spread in *Town and Country's* special 1952 Frederick & Nelson issue, retired that year after having held the post of doorman for 42 years. For decades, Seattleites would tell each other, "let's meet at Clark's door," the Sixth Avenue and Pine Street entrance. Inside the entrance was the famous book where shoppers, pre-cell phones, left each other notes about their whereabouts.

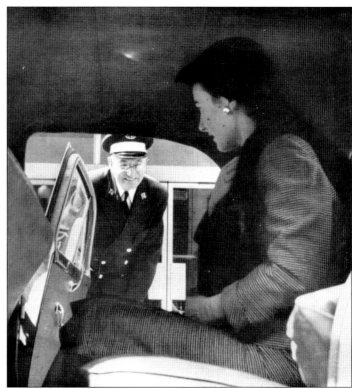

This postwar photograph, taken outside of Frederick & Nelson's, shows an increased flamboyance in fashion, as well as the abundance of specialty foods available, including the F&N gift basket. Featured in the basket was a container of Fred 'Rico Nuts, which would become a favorite of the author's family. These fancy nuts, covered half in powered sugar and half in cocoa (as well as "exotic spices"), may have even been better than Frangos.

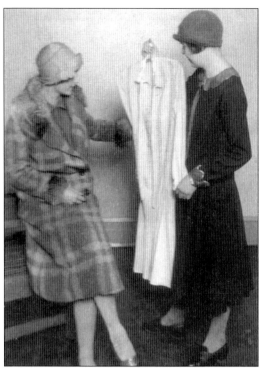

In this 1920s photograph, a Frederick & Nelson associate presents a frock to a guest for inspection. D. E. Frederick disliked the terms "salesperson" and "customer," saying he wished his staff to think of every transaction as if they were a "close friend of the customer, doing his or her very best to help the friend select the most suitable article."

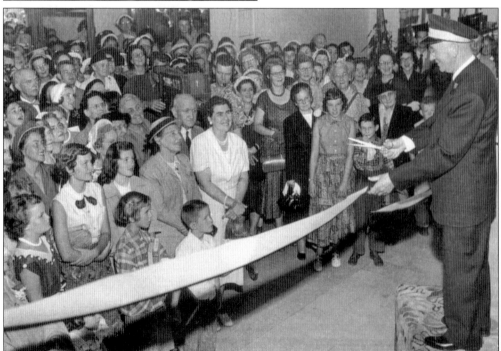

Doorman Clark Pounds cut the ribbon to officially open the remodeled store on August 4, 1952. Marshall Field's had balked at the $1.5 million price tag to air-condition the store. The day of the opening was one of the rare days that Seattle hit 90 degrees. Customers kept stopping to ask William Street what was wrong with the air-conditioning, and he soon saw to it that it was added.

The gentlemen in this photograph look stylish in their fedoras. Mrs. M. G. Porter recalled a time her husband decided to replace a hat he had bought at F&N over a year before that had never fit quite right. When she handed the clerk her Charga-Plate (a credit card predecessor), he said there was no charge because the original clerk sold the hat with a wrong fit. This "personified the customer service attitude" of her favorite store.

Alice McCallick, in the luggage department, submitted the photograph to the right for a *Between Ourselves* article about the store's 75th anniversary. It shows Alice as a child wearing a white dress purchased at Frederick's in 1910 for $12.50. Janet McLean was around Alice's age when, in 1939, her ailing mother sent her on her own to Frederick's to purchase school clothes. Her mother knew the salesladies would help her choose correctly.

It is hard to know who enjoyed the Frederick & Nelson Kindergarten most—the children happily at play or the mothers free to shop and lunch without them. Enid Toby Carnahan wrote of her memory of the hidden button for opening the Kindergarten door when her mother took her there in 1928. Twenty years later, she took her two little girls there as well to ride on the teeter-totter and play with the Lincoln Logs.

Eileen Flint remembered screaming and clutching her mother's handbag, afraid of the "Frederick's school lady," whose false teeth clicked and who smelled of orange peels. But she learned to love the school and the lady, building blocks into a fort, smearing finger paint on butcher paper, and having her mother pry her hands loose from the little piano she did not want to leave behind.

Three

EVENTS, OCCASIONS, AND SPECIAL TREATS

From its earliest days, Frederick & Nelson played an active role in the city, contributing to Seattle's arts and culture. Here is F&N's float in the first Seafair Parade. Seafair began as a plan to celebrate Seattle's centennial in 1951–1952. Conceived by prominent business leaders, including William Street, the festival was designed to attract tourists and highlight maritime events.

With what was felt to be the immediate threat to the Pacific Coast after Pearl Harbor, Frederick & Nelson's went into action to support the nation's war effort. A Victory Post was established, and bonds and stamps were sold. The store put on special events, such as exhibits, movies, and speakers, to aid bond sales, and it bought bonds with every drive.

When Frederick & Nelson launched its sixth war loan drive, it hung the two largest flags ever shown on the Pacific Coast on the outside of the building. Made especially for the store, an American flag and a "Buy War Bonds" flag, each 60-by-100 feet, covered half of each side of the building on Pine Street and Fifth Avenue.

During the fifth war loan drive, the store used 20 display windows for an elaborate and unusual display of the materials of war. Crowds jammed the streets to see these examples, secured through direct negotiations with army and navy officials. Interior displays mirrored the same subjects.

During the period of the drive, all of the store's newspaper and radio advertising was devoted to the sale of war bonds. Even the sides of the delivery trucks were pressed into service. F&N staff set themselves a goal of sponsoring a B-29 Superfortress and went on to subscribe the full amount. F&N received national recognition and special commendation from treasury officials.

A War Policy Committee was formed to coordinate activity with other civilian protection agencies. The store donated one of its delivery trucks to the auxiliary fire department, and staff members organized a defense group for protection of the store, its personnel, and customers. Here they can be seen practicing maneuvers on the store's rooftop. Red Cross first-aid classes were held at the store, and women staff members organized meetings where they rolled bandages for the Red Cross. A War Services Committee was also formed with representation from every department. One of its main activities was the enrollment of staff members in the payroll deduction plan for buying war bonds. The staff participated in a great many other wartime activities, such as staffing special shifts at the ration boards, and the women also did their part by using leg paint to simulate seams rather than buy silk stockings. (Courtesy Frederick & Nelson Records, MOHAI, Seattle.)

This photograph shows the horse-drawn float that Frederick & Nelson used when it first participated in a parade. The year is between 1893 and 1897, and it was when Silas Munro was still a partner in the business. At that time, Frederick, Nelson, and Munro was located in the Kline Building.

The Crescent was founded in 1889, and it became the spoke of Spokane's social and fashion scene. While shoppers would meet at "Clark's door" in Seattle, in Spokane, a meeting "under the clock" was understood to mean the first floor of the Crescent. Here the store can be seen in the background of the 1954 Lilac Parade.

Besides displaying merchandise, store windows were also used for civic purposes. Hundreds of people stood outside the Pine Street window to watch King 5's live broadcast of the national and local election returns in 1952. They were among the first to know that Dwight D. Eisenhower had been elected president.

The Pine Street window was also the setting for a performance in April 1969 by Franklin High School's Bel Canto Choir. The group of 100 youngsters would travel to the British Isles that summer as ambassadors of goodwill for the city of Seattle. The store had an active relationship with local teens, including sponsoring the Sub Deb Club and being an active participant in the Distributive Education Clubs of America (DECA).

Symphony conductor Sir Thomas Beecham called Seattle a "cultural dustbin" in the 1950s, and in response, Frederick & Nelson created a special window, complete with a string quartet, to publicize the Seattle Symphony Orchestra. It became a longtime sponsor of the symphony's annual Symphoneve benefit show, which is shown above being held at the Olympic hotel.

In 1965, Frederick & Nelson celebrated the store's 65th anniversary by providing a coach and team of horses as part of its theme of "An Old Fashioned Christmas." Besides the usual cast of characters, such as the Strolling Minstrels, the store debuted a new window extravaganza—a live ice-skating show.

On October 4, 1958, seven-year-old Janet Davis of Medina won the five-to-seven-year-old division of the Frederick & Nelson Hula Hoop contest. Throughout the nation that year, men, women, and especially children were caught up in the latest fad. Manufactured by Wham-O, the Hula Hoop sold for $1.98 and was so popular that stores kept running out. Wham-O sold more than 100 million Hula Hoops in the first 12 months they were on the market, and even that was not enough to meet the demand. It was reported that truckloads of the popular toys were hijacked by crazed hoopsters on their way to stores. In the above photograph, Davis is shown being able to keep four hoops in motion on her waist and one on her arm. More than 700 boys and girls, ages 5 to 15, had crowded into the usually much more sedate Tea Room over three days to compete for prizes. Winners received Frederick & Nelson gift certificates. (Courtesy Frederick & Nelson Records, MOHAI, Seattle.)

In 1968, Frederick & Nelson teamed up with United Air Lines for a promotion entitled "Discover America." Many colorful window and interior displays highlighted places to vacation, including Hawaii, the Great Lakes, and Baja, California. In addition, United Air Lines employees put on "how to pack" demonstrations in the store's resort shop. Here Roberta Talbot demonstrates space-saving techniques.

Every year the exhibition hall was home to fashion shows, classes, concerts, meetings, and other activities hosted by F&N or various art, cultural, or civic organizations. Gladys O'Donnell recalled, "We sat on folding chairs and watched a variety of wonderful shows—Japanese flower arranging, dog obedience, piano concerts, square dancing by youngsters . . . Each offering was a 'bonus.'" Hosoe Kondama, headmistress of the Ikenobo School of Flower Arrangement, is shown here.

Pictured at left with the Easter Bunny is the author's sister, Robin Wendell. A customer sent in a memory of taking her niece to the breakfast. "She hesitated shyly for only a moment, then climbed into his furry lap. The Easter Bunny asked her what she wanted for Easter. Her dark eyes widened, and she . . . pulled his long, soft ear down to her face. Into it she whispered 'you.'"

Easter Bunny breakfasts were started in 1951 and were held in the Tea Room. In 1965, admission tickets cost $1.95 for adults and $1.15 for children. Event attractions have included marionettes, accordion players, and costumed ballerinas. At the breakfast pictured in this 1979 photograph, the entertainment included Stan Boreson, a beloved local entertainer, as well as a balloon artist and juggler. The Easter Bunny and his "entourage" distributed chocolate eggs and "loads of good cheer."

Tommy Davis, popular left fielder for the Seattle Pilots (the forerunners of the Mariners), visited the book department in May 1969 to autograph copies of the book *The Tommy Davis Story* by Patrick Russell. Members of the local sports teams were frequent and popular guests. Autograph parties were also held for people as diverse as Victor Borge, James Michener, Julia Child, and Tom Robbins.

Before there was a Barnes and Noble on every corner, Frederick & Nelson was the stopping point for authors and celebrities on book tours. Pictured here in the 1970s is popular humor author Erma Bombeck, who once said, "Don't confuse fame with success. Madonna is one; Helen Keller is the other." (Courtesy Frederick & Nelson Records, MOHAI, Seattle.)

Richard Nixon visited the store on August 10, 1962, in conjunction with his book tour for *Six Crises*, which dealt with his political involvement as congressman, senator, and vice president. This political memoir examined six different crises he had experienced throughout his political career. He drew quite a crowd, and both a police and secret service presence can be seen. (Courtesy Frederick & Nelson Records, MOHAI, Seattle.)

Shown above is a special sale of silk stockings at Frederick & Nelson in 1940. An advertisement had announced the "Office of Production Management has ordered a complete stoppage of all processing of raw silk . . . To give our customers an equal opportunity to procure silk hosiery, Frederick & Nelson limits all silk hosiery purchases to six pairs to a customer, as long as our present stock lasts."

Early morning meetings kept sales staff informed about current merchandise and upcoming stock. Before any merchandise was advertised or sold, comparison shoppers would check it against store standards. And every Friday morning, before the store opened to the buying public, the coming fashion trends were demonstrated in a special fashion show that was conducted solely for the staff members of Frederick & Nelson.

The 1955 spring fashion meeting for staff opened with the latest styles by Dior and other designers modeled in the traditional fashion. Immediately after, the same fashion features were given a fresh look by the male members of the advertising department as they took to the runway. From left to right are Lex McAtee (advertising manager), John Murphy, Jim Power, Bob Fetterly, and John Lee. Ed Hansen is seated in front.

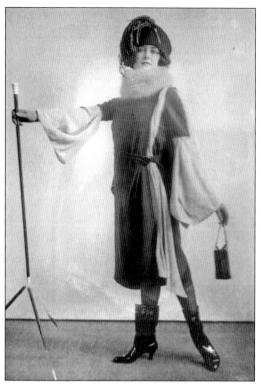

The Tea Room in the new building at Sixth Avenue and Pine Street quickly became the destination when seeking Seattle's most elegant place for lunch. Fashion shows were staged every Wednesday during fashion seasons, and a special showing of Paris originals happened twice a year. At left, model Mrs. Hamilton Douglas reveals the fall fashions of the 1920s.

The Crescent in Spokane was one year older than Frederick & Nelson, founded in 1889 by Robert Patterson and James Comstock. Marshall Field's management felt it resembled Frederick & Nelson in terms of its operation and community reputation, and purchased the store in 1969. A Crescent fashion show from the 1940s, held at the Davenport Hotel, is shown above and demonstrates the similarities between the stores.

"You girls behave yourselves or we will not go to the Tea Room today." Such was the admonition from Prudence Berlin Milligan's mother to her and her cousin Cora. The threat brought instant peace between the cousins because they knew that "only well-behaved young ladies, wearing hats and gloves, could go to tea there."

Shown here is the first "Sale of Sales" held in 1955. Offering at least a 25 percent discount on merchandise, it was one of the biggest events of its kind in the retailing world and gained the store national attention. Held in the Armory building (now the site of the Seattle Center, formerly the World's Fair grounds) it was moved to the Frederick & Nelson store in later years.

In the late 1970s and early 1980s, Frederick & Nelson, under the management of G. Arthur Henkens, made efforts to appeal to the teen market in particular. A shop called "Pzaz" was opened on the second floor with teen apparel. A hair salon, cosmetic counter, and restaurant were also added. Here is a fashion show the store cosponsored with *Seventeen* magazine.

Town and Country related that "many important things are settled in [the] . . . Tea Room every Wednesday noon. Grandchildren are discussed, social functions are planned, political leaders are applauded or maligned, recipes are exchanged . . . and all this is accomplished as smartly dressed Seattle women gather to enjoy the exceptional . . . menu and watch new fashions informally modeled . . . Many women have been meeting friends here every Wednesday for years, neatly keeping abreast of both social and fashion news simultaneously."

In 1972, the International Fashion Show was presented both at the store and at the opera house for Symphoneve. The trend-setting fashions included, in number order, a pimento and plaid pantsuit by De Rauch, a coat by Venet of Paris with a fox boa, a sapphire cigaline Dior ball gown, a coat costume from the International Collection for Day, Laroche's ivory pantsuit with fox collar and fox-trimmed ivory coat, and a jersey dress by Halston.

In 1986, then-owner Batus, Inc., agreed to sell the store to a partnership of local investors headed by Basil Vyzis, an Eastside real estate developer. The traditional Wednesday fashion shows returned to the Tea Room, but elsewhere the partners cut buying expenses, reduced staff, and converted more than 90 percent of the remaining sales associates to a commission basis.

85

Perhaps nothing evokes more memories than the Paul Bunyan room. Sylvia Wieland Nogaki and her brother loved the famous mural—little kitchen helpers skating on strips of bacon to grease Paul Bunyan's giant griddle. Ann Akers remembered "the Paul Bunyan kitchen was a favorite place to go . . . You would almost always have to wait in line to get a seat . . . There was a short little lady who was about as tall as she was wide, in a black dress with a white collar . . . her hair tied back in a bun, who would stand up on a wooden box to look over the restaurant and see when a seat would become free. She then would direct you . . . Once we were seated we didn't have to look at a menu because we always had a chicken salad sandwich and a coke followed by a hot fudge sundae made with Frango mint ice cream. The sundae was special because the hot fudge came in a separate little pitcher so that you could pour it over the ice cream yourself." (Courtesy MOHAI.)

FOR OUR YOUNG CUSTOMERS

We make a special effort to be extra helpful to young visitors in our store. Below we list a few departments specially planned for them.

OUR YOUTH FLOOR — Located on the Fourth Floor are our many young people's shops for ages from babies to teens.

BABIES — Everything for Baby from rattles to cribs, featuring famous-name brands and our own F&N labels.

GIRLS — Our Children's, Girls' and High School Shops carry styles to please young ladies at every age.

BOYS — The Children's, Boys' and Student Shops can outfit boys for play, school or dress-up time.

ACCESSORIES — Cosmetics and jewelry for the young lady plus slips, vests, panties, hosiery, handbags, etc.

TOYS — Whether it's a stuffed animal, a rag doll, or the newest rocket model, you'll find it here.

BUDGET FLOOR — Our Budget Floor . . . downstairs . . . also carries a complete selection of clothing for children.

PAUL BUNYAN

presents

Tiny Tots' MENU

Frederick & Nelson

DIVISION OF MARSHALL FIELD & COMPANY

"Crust trimmed on all sandwiches," assured the Tiny Tots' menu. Kathleen Lucas recalled that she and her brother "used to spin around on the counter stools while my Mother tried keeping those dark green F&N packages from falling!" Suze Yeasting wrote, "We would climb up to the counter and split a toasted chicken salad sandwich and a big, frosted shake . . . The waitresses reminded me of movie stars."

When the new store opened in 1918, it boasted a soda shop (the precursor to the Paul Bunyan room) that served Coca-Cola, ice cream, and cakes. June Jensen Allen remembered that she and her siblings got "25¢ or 50¢ to order a special treat" during the late 1920s. Steve Camp worked for Frederick & Nelson during the summer of 1960 and recalled that, with his employee discount, a Frango mint shake would "set me back a quarter."

The Tea Room is shown here c. 1918. Mary Louise Oakes recalled a trip to F&N in 1925 where the "grand finale" was the elegant Tea Room. "A string quartet played during the long lunch hours (although too loudly if you were seated near the musicians' platform.) The lamb with mint ice and tiny roast potatoes was bliss!" Twenty-five years later that same featured luncheon cost $1.60.

The continental buffet in the Tea Room, shown here in 1939, was a popular and quick choice. A sit down lunch might include such Tea Room specialties as chicken pot pie, Frederick & Nelson's special club sandwich, or Marshall Field's famous special salad sandwich, which boasted 1,500 served daily in Field's Tea Room.

This 1950 artist's rendering of the Tea Room in the upcoming remodel clearly shows the wide-view windows. At their customers' urging, F&N moved the Tea Room from the fifth floor to the eighth floor to ensure the best views. You could make arrangements with the hostess for an afternoon of bridge for 4 or 500, or she would direct table games at parties for the "little folks."

The oak-lined Men's Grill was also on the eighth floor and had its own, separate, "men only" entrance, cloakroom, and restroom. Wives and children were only allowed in on Wednesdays and Saturdays, and prime rib was served every day. The only other exception to the "men only" rule (other than the waitresses) was when the fashion models took a turn through the restaurant to offer some added scenery.

While ladies dined in grace and sophistication above, women below prepared their elegant cuisine in kitchens equipped with Majestic Ranges, a Frederick & Nelson exclusive. From this kitchen emerged such delicacies as "Turkey ala King on French Toast under Glass" and "Currie of Alaska King Crab in Ramekin" or simply the homey comfort of a chicken pot pie. The Frederick & Nelson kitchens were also known for their delicious baked goods. Fresh-baked rye, French rolls, and Walt's nut bread, when toasted, made the perfect foundation for a chicken or egg salad sandwich (made with Frederick & Nelson mayonnaise, of course). In the Paul Bunyan room, a customer might have a slice of Olympic Berry Pie, while the Tea Room had its own eponymous Layer Cake. The treat the author remembers best is the cinnamon rolls, with wafer thin layers that wrapped round and round to come to a tip. She used to see if she could unwrap one in a single long curl before devouring it. (Courtesy Frederick & Nelson Records, MOHAI, Seattle.)

Oscar Skau (above) was known as "Mr. Ice Cream" and supervised the production of all Frederick & Nelson ice creams and Frango frozen desserts. One treat was Olympic Berry Sherbet, made from berries grown exclusively for Frederick & Nelson on Vashon Island. The author recently met with gardener Kathy Mendelson, who had obtained a secret cache of the berry starts and felt a bit as if she had scored a major connection. June Jensen Allen remembers visiting the soda fountain in the 1920s and watching them make all those "concoctions." These included sundaes with names such as Jack and Jill, Fairy Land, Dusky Dream, and Chocolate Soldier. Another specialty staff member was Eddie Elliott, probably the only person in the country who could accurately reproduce a photographic portrait on a cake using vegetable coloring. He was an artist before becoming a baker at Frederick & Nelson and also reproduced landscapes and cartoons on cake icing. It took 21 operations to ice the average cake, and some made-to-order cakes cost up to $50 in the late 1940s.

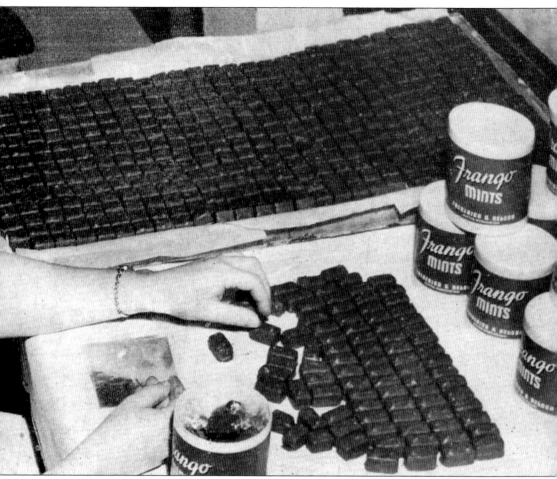

Jeffrey Foster recalled, "Every year at Christmas time, my mother would buy a box of Frango mints from Frederick & Nelson for guests who might drop by during the holidays. My older brother and I were crazy about Frango mints but weren't allowed to have any. Fortunately for us, the box had two layers so we would lift up the top layer and sneak one or two from the bottom. When we began to make a big dent in the bottom layer, we would combine the two layers into one. Nowadays my wife buys the Frango mints and hides them somewhere—where I wish I knew. I still eat 'em from the bottom." Although Frangos were Frederick & Nelson's best-known candies, over the years, the store produced more than 400 different varieties. A customer wrote of a visit around the beginning of the 20th century when she still remembers "the candy counter, chock full of salt water taffy and nutty clusters and yummy dark chocolate."

In the 1940s, Frederick & Nelson operated the largest handmade candy factory in the United States. At that time, it was located on Fourteenth Avenue and Washington Street. When Frangos were first made, the chocolate candy was cooked and then poured onto tables to cool. Then it was cut into bite-sized mints and hand finished.

This scene on the Frango mint assembly line in 1951 appears calm and orderly, but for an inexperienced worker, it could easily turn into the famous *I Love Lucy* scene where Lucy and Ethel resort to stuffing chocolates in their pockets, hats, and mouths as they come down the line at a furious pace. The author's sister still will not speak of her summer at the Frango factory.

Jean Cook of Whitehorse, Yukon Territory, wrote to F&N in 1979, saying, "we see many . . . commercials from Seattle and one that has finally piqued my curiosity to the point of finding your address and writing to you is a candy commercial [for Frangos] . . . They sound absolutely delicious and I would like to . . . order some by mail . . . your commercials reach communities thousands of miles from you and . . . the items are of great appeal."

By 1990, the F&N candy kitchen, located on the 10th floor of the downtown store, produced more than 4,200 pounds of Frango mints daily to meet the holiday demand. Shown above is Angela Valentine at the weighing machine. Jeanne Hsu remembers her family always buying boxes of Frangos at Christmas. She wrote to the author, "They had just mint chocolate in those days, and they were wrapped so festively."

Frango Triple-Treat Chocolate Layer Cake

6 Frango Mint dark chocolates, chopped fine
2 ounces unsweetened chocolate, chopped fine
1/2 cup boiling water
2 1/2 cups sifted cake flour
1/4 cup unsweetened nonalkalized cocoa powder
1 tspn. baking soda

1/2 tspn. salt
1 cup (2 sticks) unsalted butter, softened
2 cups granulated sugar
4 large eggs, at room temperature
3/4 tspn. pure vanilla extract
1 cup buttermilk

Place the rack in the center of the oven and preheat the oven to 350° F. Generously butter three 9-inch round layer cake pans. Line the bottom of each with a circle of waxed paper. Lightly butter the paper.

Put the Frango Mints and unsweetened chocolate in the small bowl . Add the boiling water and stir until smooth. Let cool to room temperature.

Sift together the cake flour, cocoa, baking soda, and salt. set aside.

With an electric mixer on medium speed, beat the butter until smooth. Gradually add the sugar and increase to high speed. Continue beating about 2 minutes until mixture is light and fluffy. Add the eggs, one at at time, mixing well after each addition. Mix in vanilla and chocolate mixture. Alternately add the buttermilk and dry ingredients, adding about one-third at a time, beginning with buttermilk.

In 2004, Kimberly Carsberg was shopping in Bon-Macy's in downtown Seattle and came upon a woman handing out recipes from Toni Keene, the store's chef, which described various ways to use "our trademark Frango Chocolates." The emphasis was no doubt intentional, as Bon-Macy's had only recently ended a legal battle over Frangos that included rights to the name, recipe, and even the classic hexagonal box, and involved, at various times, six different companies. The recipes included such tempting treats as Frango crispy shortbread, chunky Frango ice cream, Frangomellos, and ooey gooey chewy Frango brownies, but it was the recipe for Frango triple-treat chocolate layer cake, reproduced above complete with chocolate smudges, that proved the biggest hit at the Carsberg family Christmas party that year.

Divide the batter among the prepared pans. Bake for 15 minutes. Rearrange the pans in the oven from front to back so they bake evenly. Continue baking 15 to 20 minutes longer, until a toothpick inserted in the center comes out clean. Let the cakes cool in the pan for 10 minutes. Loosen from the pans and invert onto a wire rack. Peel off the waxed paper and cool completely.

Frosting

12 Fango Mint dark chocolates, chopped fine
2 ounces unsweetened chocolate, chopped fine

2 1/4 cups (4 1/2 sticks) unsalted butter, softened
1 cup plus 2 tablespoons confectioners' sugar, sifted

15 Frango Mint dark chocolates, chopped fine

For the frosting, melt the Frango Mints and chocolate in the top of a double boiler over simmering water, stirring until smooth. Set aside to cool.

With an electric mixer, beat the butter until smooth. Gradually add the cooled chocolate. Add the confectioners' sugar and beat until smooth.

Invert one layer onto a cake plate. Smooth about 1 cup frosting over it. Top with another layer and frost. Add top layer, upside down. Evenly frost the top and sides of the cake with the remaining frosting. Sprinkle the cake with additional chopped Frango Mints.

Makes 1 9-inch layer cake.

Recipe from "Someone's in the Kitchen with DayTon's Marshall Fields Hudson's" Contemporary Books ©1993 Dayton

Above c. 1990, local television personalities Jeff Renner (left) and Tony Ventrella (right) demonstrated their culinary talents (not causing the future Rachel Ray to lose any sleep) at the cooking school in F&N's basement, then called the Arcade. Until 1981, this had been the bargain basement where even Seattleites such as Harriet Bullitt, the daughter of one of the country's wealthiest families and heir to the King broadcasting fortune, would browse.

The 1990s version of the famous Frango ice cream sundae is held by Mauricio Oliva, an associate in the Arcade Café, which, as thousands of longtime Frederick's fans knew, did not hold a candle to the Paul Bunyan room. The Frango mint sauce, sadly pooling in its plastic tub instead of streaming proudly from its silver pitcher, was a harbinger of the end.

Four

CHRISTMAS AND THE ONE TRUE SANTA

Here is the front cover of the December 1955 *Between Ourselves*. The inside cover shares a letter from William Street that says, in part, " we provide just the stage and are ourselves only the stagehands. The customers are . . . the stars, they make the performance and give to it their great feeling about the holidays. We are deeply moved each year by the . . . holiday mood and affection our customers share with us."

The amount of display materials and staff hours used in creating the holiday displays staggered the imagination. Artists and designers began even before the previous year's trim had been taken down. One year, the display department constructed 45 chandeliers with 15,000 plastic prisms, used 811 yards of satin, strung 25,000 feet of gold beads, and used 18,000 ornaments and 15,000 lights in garlands and trees.

By October, all display shops were in full swing, creating every detail of that year's trim. While one shop might perform miracles with hammers, nails, saws, and paint, the staff at the Seventh Avenue and Olive Way building would keep sewing machines humming and fingers flying, creating a plethora of decorative accessories. Others focused on creating beautiful and creative wrappings for hundreds of display packages.

Here customers are browsing during the 1936 Christmas season. With the Depression sweeping the nation, Frederick's finances improved gradually during the mid-1930s, and by 1936, the store recorded $7,870,934 in sales—an improvement but still only half of its earnings prior to 1929. D. E. Frederick, the store's founder, would pass away the following year. In the early days of the store, he would stroll through the departments, wishing season's greetings to all.

Even while war raged in Europe during the 1940s, Frederick & Nelson was packed with holiday shoppers. Clara Magnussen recalled the "lovely walnut showcases filled with exquisite merchandise, enhanced by the gorgeous red and gold decor of Christmastime." F&N president William Street reminded staff that while "our assortments of merchandise have been the largest ever . . . the real warmth of the store still remains in our personal reception to each individual customer."

During the 1958 Christmas season, Jeanne Case (right) was one of the Frederick & Nelson associates who worked the "stag line," where gentlemen of all ages could seek assistance with their Christmas shopping. At left is Kim Estrada, who is choosing a present for his mother, Evalyn Mitchell, an assistant buyer in the children's shoes department. That year, a multicolored ribbon theme was used throughout the store, inspiring many compliments.

There were several departments that existed just for the holiday season, including trim-a-tree, Christmas tree lane, and, of course, gift wrapping. At right, presents are awaiting delivery in their green foil and red ribbon wrapping. June Jensen Allen's father worked for F&N for 36 years. She recalled "Christmas time deliveries were always exciting for . . . us kids. Big boxes of many sizes arrived via F&N trucks. Dad was a wonderful shopper."

In 1958, mail shopping manager Rachel Witter (left) and packing room manager Linden Hardman (right) checked an order being sent to radar stations at the Arctic Circle, reversing the usual process of packages arriving from the North Pole. The package, containing tablecloths, favors, and centerpieces for a Christmas dinner, had to be specially packed to be dropped by parachute.

The poem to the right appeared in the November/December 1965 *Between Ourselves*, reprinted from an earlier issue. It was one of the few times that some of the challenges of dealing with the public in a retail setting were addressed, even in this humorous fashion. More common were statements like William Street's, that the quality of F&N's service stems from "our scrupulous adherence to the highest of standards . . . accompanied with utmost courtesy and helpfulness."

"A Department Store Salesgirl's Visit from Saint Nicholas"

'Twas the night before Christmas, and all through the flat
Not a creature was stirring (include me in that).
My stockin's, a little the worse for tough wear,
Were flung on the back of a three-legged chair.

Outside—snow was falling in beautiful flakes,
But I didn't care, I was too full of aches.
I'd worked in the store through the holiday strife
And was plannin' to sleep for the rest of my life.

When all of a sudden I hear rumpus and clatter,
So I leaps out of bed to see what was the matter.
(I thought at the time 'twas the nut down one flight
Who starts up his radio late every night.)

So I opened the window and loudly did cry:
"Hey, is this Christmas Eve or the Fourth of July?"
And what to my dead-with-sleep eyes should appear
But a hinky-dink sleigh and eight tiny reindeer;

And who should be drivin' right up to the door
But one of them masquerade guys from the store.
I said to myself, what can be this guy's game?
When he clucked to his reindeer and called them by name.

Well, I'd never observed these store actors much;
I had thought they was Yanks, but this feller talked Dutch.
And just as I'm dopin' out what next he would do,
Right up to a housetop the whole outfit flew.

And then in a twinklin' I heard on the roof
The prancin' and pawin' of meat on the hoof.
(Just imagine my feelin's, for sleep nearly dead
And a nut with an animal show overhead.)

As I drew in my bean and was turnin' around
Down the chimney my visitor came with a bound.
A big bag of junk he displayed with a grin,
And he acted to me like he'd come to move in.

The stump of a pipe graced his jaw as he spoke
And asked, "Got a match? Do you mind if I smoke?"
He had a broad face and (pardon me) belly
That shook when he laughed like a bowl full of jelly.

He was chubby, good natured, and oozin' with glee;
But I ask you, dear reader, what was that to me?
The point that I make, 'twas then two o'clock
And a guy in my room without stoppin to knock.

I was thinkin' how noisy he was and how slick,
When he says to me, "LADY, I'M ONLY ST. NICK."
Well—a poor, tired store girl's in no mood for fun,
So I gives him a look and asked him, "Which one?"

"As a Christmas-rush salesgirl," I says, "you'll agree
That a look at St. Nick ain't no big treat to me.
This has gone far enough and this bunk's gotta stop;
Take the air with them goats or I'll yell for a cop!"

He said not a word, but went on with his work
And filled up my stockin's, then turned with a jerk;
And layin' a finger aside his red nose,
And givin' a nod, up the chimney he rose.

He sprang to his sleigh with a shake of his head
And I pulled the shades down and flopped into bed.
"Merry Christmas," he called, as away his deers ran—
And I just gave him a yawn and said, "So's your old man!"

101

The contrast between a Christmas Catalog from 1915 and one from 1965 is shown here. The 16-page, 1915 catalog included such best sellers as a celluloid Kewpie doll for 75¢, and a pair of 16-button white kid gloves for $2.65. Both invited out-of-town friends to visit the store, to "make it a meeting place for friends, check their luggage, and avail themselves of all the store's facilities."

In 1963, the courtesy car that shuttled between F&N and the Olympic Hotel was a festively wrapped Volkswagen bus. The green ribbon on the blue car matched the awning under which doorman Donald Hinze stood in his traditional green uniform. Victor Rosellini, noted Seattle restaurateur, recalled in a 1992 *Seattle Times* article that if your packages missed the last truck, they would be sent to your house in a cab.

In 1948, the store itself was a wrapped present, complete with gift tag. A customer wrote, "I try to pay my account with Frederick's, but I am sure I can never repay my whole indebtedness. I think the city of Seattle owes a debt to your great store. Frederick & Nelson is a constant source of pleasure and satisfaction to me and never more so than at this Christmas season."

The decoration of F&N was a magnet drawing people downtown. One customer wrote, "Thank you—to you and your staff, on giving Seattle and its many families such pleasure at this time of year. Our family has made a lot of trips downtown just to look at your store. One can't help but feel you are in the center of fairyland. You are truly an asset to Seattle."

Sylvia Wieland Nogaki wrote in the *Seattle Times* in 1992 that "it has become a cliché to say that Christmas isn't Christmas without Frederick & Nelson. But it was true . . . when everyone seemed to be living in ramblers and eating Kraft macaroni and cheese . . . Frederick's was an elegant home away from home, where a little girl could dream of red velvet dresses with lace collars, and oversized, stuffed rabbits with long, floppy ears."

"It's a Beautiful White Christmas at Frederick & Nelson" was the holiday theme for the 75th anniversary year. There were 50,000 tiny lights, thousands of glistening snowflakes, and delicate white branches arched over the red-carpeted aisles. Shown above is the Fifth Avenue and Pine Street corner window as a fairyland of snow.

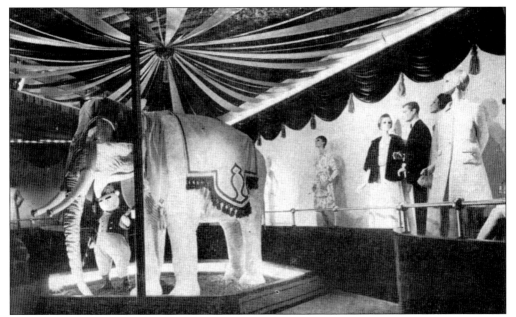

Christmas 1968 saw a circus performing in the Pine Street window with an accordion-playing lion and the elephant, pictured above. The elephant looked so real that many passersby did a double take, and one little girl was heard to say, "Ssh, he's going to talk now." Sylvia Wieland Nogaki recalled the animated window displays, especially a Santa's workshop where "an elf slowly raised and lowered a tiny hammer."

The tradition of in-store caroling by the staff chorus, shown here performing in a store window around 1958, was first established in 1918. Every morning for the five days before Christmas, customers would gather to hear the choral society sing carols under the first floor clock for the first 10 minutes after the store opened. For years, this was broadcast live on local radio station KRSC.

During wartime, children still found pleasure in looking into F&N's toy-filled window. By 1952, children had a special adventure when display director Joe Sjurgen found a way to power a toy train by pressing a hand on the window. The technology of power derived from body heat, developed by the navy and rendered through Sjurgen's imagination, was truly magical.

A particular signature of F&N's innovative window displays was the use of live animals, including reindeer, polar bears, sheep, penguins, seals, rabbits, and flamingos. Sjurgen reassured the public that the Seattle Humane Society had been consulted, and that "we do everything we can to make them happy." The penguins pictured here certainly appear to have happy feet.

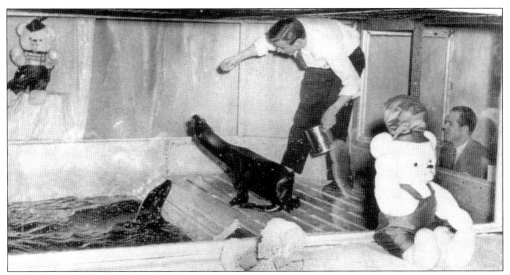

William Street felt that Joe Sjurgen was "the one person who most affected the public's visual perception of Frederick & Nelson" by designing functional displays that encouraged audience involvement. Customers would consistently write in with their praise, including comments such as, "This year tops *everything*!" and "This year you have outdone yourself. What are you going to do for an encore? . . . Absolutely magnificent!"

Having Alaskan reindeer in the window proved to be a considerable challenge. Unused to Seattle's warmer climate, the reindeer began losing their hair in great chunks, and Hugh Mann, vice president of visual presentation, recalled they "had to glue it back on. Then the antlers fell off, and we tried gluing them on. When that did not work, we strapped them on with harnesses." Twenty-five years later, they were more successful with reindeer raised in Oregon.

Joe Sjursen told the *Seattle Post-Intelligencer* that most of the animals used in displays were "extroverts and like to show off. When we had flamingos, which are supposed to hide behind things, they were in full view all the time." Douglass Welch, a local newspaper columnist, described the display department as "the artist and the mechanic, at once imaginative and practical."

This 1955 postcard carries the caption, "In Seattle, Christmas isn't Christmas without a Day at Frederick & Nelson. Seattle's most beautiful department store has rolled out the red carpet for its friends and neighbors this Christmas. The scene shows one of the first floor aisles." The red carpet was matched by the posts wrapped in red satin, each of which served as a background for a lit and decorated tree.

The Delicacy Shop is shown here in 1965. The famous Frederick & Nelson gift baskets could be found here, full of exotic and delicious edibles. In 1962, for the Seattle World's Fair, the Delicacy Shop followed suit by honoring various nations on special days. The shop displayed and promoted the food of each country and decorated the department with the colors and images associated with the individual country. In some cases, native costumes were worn. Some of the countries included were Denmark, Italy, France, Germany, and Great Britain. Abe Liu remembers, "F&N had a gourmet food section before it became fashionable to offer gourmet foods. I remember when, in college, someone I knew bought a can of French fried ants (or maybe they were French fried grasshoppers or chocolate-covered ants . . . I don't really remember that clearly, but I do remember that they were bugs) as a joke gift. F&N was the only store that offered such stuff."

In 1968, the mall entrance of the Southcenter store received its first holiday trim. Southcenter was the first enclosed mall in the Pacific Northwest. During the 1960s, tens of thousands of newcomers were moving to the area, due in large part to the expansion of Boeing, which was developing the 747. Most of these new arrivals lived in suburban areas.

This postcard from the 1960s shows a change from the usual red carpet to green. The chandeliers were decorated with greenery, and the trees were white. One Christmas in the 1960s, the display department sent a scale model tree decorated in that year's trim to Vietnam, where a staff member's son was stationed. When it arrived, soldiers came from miles around to experience this taste of home.

Santa's graceful white reindeer flew overhead in this photograph of the Aurora Village store. Santa's sleigh and reindeer were built, painted, and decorated by hand in the display shop. Howard Porter, responsible for creating the nativity set that hung above the first floor elevators in the main store, would return to work in the display shop every Christmas, even after moving to Oregon.

The winter wonderland theme of 1965 prompted the following complimentary letter from a customer: "A must on my list of things to do is a visit to Frederick & Nelson . . . decorations, glittering and tasteful, bring back childhood memories no longer evoked by this commercial age. I send you my greetings with a Thank You for retaining the beauty and dignity this time should have."

In 1971, the first floor was opulent in gold and white, accented by hundreds of sparkling snowflakes. Forty thousand doilies were first fireproofed, then hand-dipped in gold paint for the snowflakes and cone trees. One hundred and fifty gallons of paint were used in three days. One hundred live trees were painted gold as well and strung with lights.

The Strolling Minstrels were a Frederick & Nelson Christmas tradition. The group was headed by popular Seattle musician Frank Sugia, who lead and played his accordion in the store for more than 25 years. Here the Minstrels were shown against the English pine paneling of the old world shop on the seventh floor.

The annual Uncle Mistletoe and Santa Claus breakfasts began at the downtown store in 1951 and quickly became a tradition with Washington families. Approximately 650 parents and children attended each one. Entertainment was provided by the Strolling Minstrels, Nutcracker ballet dancers, and, in the case of the 1970 breakfast at Aurora Village pictured above, Gertrude from the local J. P. Patches television show.

The Santa breakfasts were envisioned as family parties. For most children, the food served was definitely secondary. Children would sit in small circles and sing holiday songs with members of the Dorothy Fisher Junior Ballet. Another frequent activity, shown here, was a game of London Bridge. And, of course, the biggest thrill was to have Santa come right to your table to visit.

Santa could not wait for the summer of 1963 opening of the Aurora Village store, so he set up housekeeping in the Cozy Cloud Cottage in the mall during the holiday season of 1962. That year, he was photographed with hundreds of eager children who lived north of Seattle.

Frederick & Nelson created its own cast of holiday characters unique to the store. In this 1954 photograph, Aunt Holly visits with Pamela Jean Allyn (left) and Raymond Frederick Allyn Jr. (right). Adam Woog, another faithful F&N customer, related a story from the same time where he had a screaming tantrum at the idea of wearing short pants for a visit to F&N. (Courtesy Allyn family.)

Uncle Mistletoe was the male counterpart to Aunt Holly. In this 1953 photograph he is shown with the Swanson girls, Lynne (left) and Diane (right) in their matching outfits. Lynne remembers visiting with Uncle Mistletoe before going to see Santa. Apparently, Uncle Mistletoe acted as the St. Peter of the Santa system, determining whether or not you had been good enough to move on to Santa. In 1955, Uncle Mistletoe and Aunt Holly moved into their new Cozy Cloud Cottage in Toyland on the fourth floor of the downtown store. It was never entirely clear if Aunt Holly and Uncle Mistletoe were married or just "cottaging up" together. There were eventually Cozy Cloud Cottages at all the suburban stores. In 1971, the Bellevue Cozy Cloud Cottage featured a tree decorated entirely with dolls. (Courtesy Lynne Dauenhauer and Diane Murray families.)

In 1943, Joe Sjursen put Santa Claus in the Sixth Avenue and Pine Street window so children could visit and tell him what they wanted for Christmas. Art French, photographer for the *Seattle Post-Intelligencer*, came up with the idea of photographing this activity. He started Arthur and Associates Holiday Photographers, which is still in business today. Pictured here are Sandra Allyn (left) and Linda Allyn (right) in 1947. (Courtesy Allyn family.)

In 1951, Lynne Swanson visited Santa with her white fur muff and fur-trimmed hooded coat, purchased perhaps at F&N. Another customer wrote of her own holiday outfit, recalling "the red coat with velvet collar and cuffs and a wonderful stylish flare at the hem. My red coat from Frederick & Nelson. I never have, before or since, felt quite so grand a lady." (Courtesy Lynne Dauenhauer and Diane Murray families.)

A photographic souvenir of a trip to visit Santa was a treasured item for many families. The photographs came packaged in a cardboard foldout frame like this one with appropriate graphics decorating the front or inside page facing the photograph. The photographs would sit with pride on the family mantel, stockings hung with care below. (Courtesy White family.)

While many children believed the one true Santa spent the time before his Christmas Eve sleigh ride at the downtown Frederick & Nelson and all other Santa's were, at best, "helpers" and, at worst, imposters, some suburban youth believed the real Santa was at their local Cozy Cloud Cottage. Here Bruce White, aged four and a half years old, visits the Bellevue Santa in 1951. (Courtesy White family.)

At left is a drawing of the F&N holiday music makers, the Strolling Minstrels. The group was lead by Frank Sugia on the accordion, Gary Steele on bass fiddle, and sometimes joined by jazz great Joe Venuti on violin. In later years, the lineup included Rolley Morehouse on clarinet and Floyd Standifer on trumpet. Their image was frequently on Santa picture folders, as were Uncle Mistletoe and Aunt Holly. (Courtesy Allyn family.)

The entire Allyn family, or at least the child contingent, were present for this 1952 Santa photograph. Pictured left to right are (standing) Linda Rae and Sandra; (seated) Raymond Frederick Jr. and baby Pamela Jean, resting her hand on Santa's belly, which no doubt shook like a bowlful of jelly. (Courtesy Allyn family.)

The Swanson girls are back for their annual Santa photograph in 1952. Lynne is at left and Diane is at right. No matching outfits this year, but they are bundled up for a Seattle winter day. The weather that Christmas season was strikingly unremarkable, although temperatures at the same time the year before had reached a record low of 10 degrees. (Courtesy Lynne Dauenhauer and Diane Murray families.)

Diane Swanson (left) grew up to work at F&N in lingerie on the budget floor from 1969 to 1977. Her sister Lynne, (right) started work at F&N as a retailing student in 1966, her senior year of high school. She spent one Christmas as a merchandising supervisor in the toy department— not her favorite experience. (Courtesy Lynne Dauenhauer and Diane Murray families.)

Pamela Jean Allyn gets Santa all to herself in 1956. *Between Ourselves* summed up the Santa experience as follows one year: "Christmas at Frederick & Nelson is . . . a place where mommy takes me all dressed up . . . a window full of trains and cars that go whoosh . . . Raggedy Ann and friends flying in Santa's sleigh . . . telling the *real* Santa Claus what you *really* wanted most in all the big, wide world."

In 1956, all Diane Swanson, (left) pictured with sister, Lynn, (right) wanted was "her two front teeth." Donald Gardner wrote "All I Want for Christmas Is My Two Front Teeth" in 1944 while teaching music at a public school in Smithtown, New York. He asked the class what they wanted for Christmas, and noticed that almost all had at least one front tooth missing. (Courtesy Lynne Dauenhauer and Diane Murray families.)

Linda and Julie Croasdill, aged four months, made their Christmas debut with the F&N Santa in 1962. Big brother, Kevin, (left) seems happy with the whole affair, but younger brother, Gregg, (right) appears at bit unsure. Kevin, Gregg, Linda, and Julie were the children of Dave Croasdill of the display department, and this picture appeared in the December 1962 issue of *Between Ourselves*.

The author has her moment with Santa Claus in this photograph taken in 1962. Her father's 35 percent employee discount no doubt influenced the amount of toys Santa left under her tree, which helped make her house the envy of neighborhood children. Another factor was the backyard play equipment, built from F&N display discards, including a stand-up sandbox like the one in the store's Kindergarten.

"A child's small fingers pressed against the glass; the look of wonder that lights his face as he observes the legendary figure of Saint Nicholas, somehow embody much of the joy that is Christmas." This photograph from the December 1971 *Between Ourselves* shows a father and son looking in the window at Sixth Avenue and Pine Street at Santa at work. Santa's helper stands to the right.

In this 1975 photograph, Sarah White pays a visit to Santa at the downtown store. She is four and a half, the same age as her father, Bruce White, when he was photographed with the Bellevue Square Santa in 1951. In all likelihood, she is sitting on the lap of Santa Paul (Paul Sinar) who became the downtown store Santa in the early 1960s and remained so for more than 30 years. (Courtesy White family.)

Shown here is Sean Dauenhauer, regarding Santa with deep suspicion in 1976. He may be on the lap of Santa Seaborn. Seaborn worked for some 20 years at the Bellevue F&N and learned sign language for the deaf children who came to see him. Hazel Viydo and her late husband, Kenneth, bought the photography business in 1962 after the death of Art French. (Courtesy Lynne Dauenhauer and Diane Murray families.)

In 1977, Sean Dauenhauer (left) is joined by his brother Kevin (right). The boys are Lynne (Swanson) Dauenhauer's children, who worked at F&N until the birth of Sean. She worked in the record department on the ninth floor, which also housed the television department. She remembers chairs being put out during the World Series so husbands could watch the games while their wives shopped. (Courtesy Lynne Dauenhauer and Diane Murray families.)

In 1978, the Dauenhauer boys return—Sean (left) and Kevin (right). Loyal McMillen is a daughter of the Nordstrom dynasty but still took her five children to F&N every year to see Santa. She recalled how "the baby would always cry, and we'd use the picture as our Christmas card." It might have looked something like the picture to the left. (Courtesy Lynne Dauenhauer and Diane Murray families.)

This 1989 photograph shows the Swanson girls all grown up and with children of their own. Seated is Joe Brown, son of Diane (Murray) Brown. From left to right are (second row) Kevin Dauenhauer and his mother, Lynne (Swanson) Dauenhauer; (third row) Sean Dauenhauer, Heather Brown, and Diane (Murray) Brown, daughter of Diane (Swanson) Murray. The family visited the F&N Santa for 38 years. (Courtesy Lynne Dauenhauer and Diane Murray families.)

Santa Claus graced the Frederick & Nelson window at Sixth Avenue and Pine Street for the last time in 1991. Once the photographs were developed, the employees of Arthur and Associates would package the pictures in Hazel Viydo's basement, guided by the energetic Hazel Viydo herself. They had a million stories to tell, including a woman who was photographed with her pet snake wrapped around her.

Frederick & Nelson

THE MAGIC OF CHRISTMAS IS IN THE GIVING

1991

Santa Paul was at the downtown store for the last time in 1991. On his knee sits the author's daughter, Isabelle Burke, aged nine months old, having her first Santa photograph taken. In 2001, Santa Paul "went north to feed his reindeer" for the last time. One family revealed that, for the last 24 years, he had gone to their home on Christmas Eve to visit their special needs daughter.

After Frederick & Nelson closed in 1992, the Viydos set up operation in Westlake Center, Southcenter, the Everett Mall, and Lamonts stores at Northgate, Alderwood, Lake Forest Park, Totem Lake, and SeaTac. Each year they shoot tens of thousands of photographs of youngsters posing with St. Nick. Santa Paul moved to the Lamonts store in Northgate, and in this 1992 photograph, again had Isabelle Burke on his lap.

A friend of the late Santa Paul recalled that he had convinced Woodland Park Zoo to let him pose with some local reindeer. "On Christmas Eve, because of the long lines outside the F&N Santa window, lots of people missed their chance of getting their Santa picture taken. So he'd venture outside to wish everyone a Merry Christmas, and he'd show the kids his album with the reindeer pictures."

Merry Christmas
To All
And To All
A Good Night

"I remember the wood inside the Frederick's elevators. And those dazzling lights we didn't have in Bremerton. It was the ultimate in luxury. The feel of it, and the smell of it. It smelled . . . like money."

—Kaaren Mynar Netwig, longtime customer

"Whatever they did, they did with class. The customer was always right."

—Victor Rosellini, local restaurateur

"It was not just a store. It was an institution, a cold word for cherished places that shape our lives."

—Sylvia Wieland Nogaki, *Seattle Times* reporter

"Still, like an old sweet song, Frederick's clings to the synapses of many longtime Puget Sounders. It evokes gone but not forgotten events in their lives . . . a sense of something lost—a child in a velvet-collared Chesterfield coat sitting on Santa's knee. A friend, a first formal, a taste of elegance or innocence."

—Susan Paynter, *Seattle Post-Intelligencer* reporter

ACROSS AMERICA, PEOPLE ARE DISCOVERING SOMETHING WONDERFUL. *THEIR HERITAGE.*

Arcadia Publishing is the leading local history publisher in the United States. With more than 4,000 titles in print and hundreds of new titles released every year, Arcadia has extensive specialized experience chronicling the history of communities and celebrating America's hidden stories, bringing to life the people, places, and events from the past. To discover the history of other communities across the nation, please visit:

www.arcadiapublishing.com

Customized search tools allow you to find regional history books about the town where you grew up, the cities where your friends and family live, the town where your parents met, or even that retirement spot you've been dreaming about.